CODING

WITH

PYTHON

An Introductory Guide for Beginners to Learn and Start Coding with Python

CHRISTOPHER WILKINSON

Table of Contents

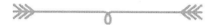

Introduction

We live in a digital world, where technology has become the most important feature in our everyday lives. And we're not just talking about the wheel. Everywhere you look, you are surrounded by a digital ecosystem that draws you in, holds you tight, and changes your life forever. Whether you're chatting on your phone, playing a game, or sending an important email to your clients, the mesh of software and hardware has become an integral part of our existence.

One of the most prominent advances lies in how we integrate the digital world into everything we do. Your phone has become a one-stop for all. Your shopping lists and financial management can be done easily with a few apps. Entertainment is slowly moving away from shooting hoops with the boys to playing tennis on your game console. Social anxiety is being solved through instant messaging. Teams work together online, no longer held down by the need for a physical working space. Whatever you want to buy can be delivered straight to your door after browsing through an online catalog. And if you're stuck for information, you have the handy web browser that will bombard you with everything you need – and don't.

It's a brave new world, and everything is changing at a radically fast pace. We do everything we can to keep up, of course, and we try our bests to be a part of this new frontier. To do this, we need to understand that everything this digital world has to offer can be broken down into one word: CODE.

Yup, the code. No, this is not a blue pill/red pill scenario, and you aren't trapped in some warped version of the Matrix (or are you?). The truth of the matter is that everything around us, everything we use to get through our days, is based on a seemingly complex set of rules and numbers. Your apps, your browser, the games you play. When you break them down, they're all a myriad of codes grouped together to give you the final product you use.

And who wouldn't want to be part of that? Who wouldn't love to be an architect of their own little corner of this digital universe? Believe us when we tell you that it isn't as hard as you think. All you really need to do is know the language and its intricacies, then start building away.

When it comes to language, this is one of the most useful books you can have in your arsenal of knowledge. It will take you, step by step, down the road of how to code, and most importantly, think like a programmer. We will be using Python 3.7.4, which is the latest version at the time of release. All you need to do is get yourself a nice cup of coffee (or tea, if that's your preference), a computer and an internet connection. Follow the steps we will outline here, and in no time, you will impress your boss, friends and family members. You'll feel like a God on 'a digital' earth.

Spoiler alert! Once people start seeing the kind of magic that you are able to do, favors will not stop haunting you. The only advice we can give you is not to reveal your super powers to just anyone. If you happen to have an alias, this is the time to use it.

This book covers all of the small stuff as well, like installing Python properly and installing a suitable editor. You get to learn about basic programming concepts that are used with all programming languages, like data types, arithmetic operations and loops. Later in the book, you will learn about functions and how to create abstractions in your code. Also, concepts like local versus global scopes, exception handling, and how to properly comment and document your code will be made a lot clearer. Deeper down the rabbit hole, you will learn how to manipulate excel and PDF files that automate an extremely tedious process. Imagine having the ability to add or delete a certain excel row or cell in hundreds of files within mere seconds. You will also be able to add watermarks to all of those PDFs you have saved in file.

Who is this book for?

This book is designed for the absolute beginner; the underdog we're rooting for and know will eventually come out on top. We will be going through everything bit by bit, in as much details as possible, so you can be assured that your first steps down this supposedly frightening journey feel like a walk in the park. We have also added illustrations, images and plenty of code for you to explore. So, if you have no programming background, then that is actually great. Choosing to start with Python as a language is a great choice.

In principle, to be fluent in a language like Python, it would take you two to three months of coding for a couple of hours a day. If you plan to use what you've learned and apply it to a career, you will need to learn more advanced specializations. That normally takes a year, if you code two to three hours a day. Since you are here and reading this, we assume that you have a specific intention in mind as to why you want to learn this language. Whatever it may be, we assure you that once you get started, your educational journey will only get better and you may end up doing a lot more with the language than you thought you could.

Just do us a favor and try not to take over the world.

What is programming?

In short, programming is the act of writing a program with a sequence of statements and procedures that are interpreted by a computer. In simple terms, programming is the act of creating programs. To create programs, you need to have a sequence of ideas that are going to be interpreted by the computer.

Let's say you want to create a program that will be able to add two numbers. The normal sequence a programmer would think about is this:

 i.   We need somewhere to store the first number

 ii. We need somewhere to store the second number

 iii. We need somewhere to store the sum

 iv. We need to let the computer know that we want to add the numbers and store it at the resulting "place".

Although it may seem like this is a simple task and can feel like 'over-engineering', it really isn't. When you build a program, you should always keep the bigger picture and big idea in mind. One of those ideas is scalability. This can be shown easily when we talk about the years leading to the millennium when there was a great hype in the computer world.

In the early nineties, the millennium bug was talked about in every enterprise that operated computers. This was an inherent bug in the computers that could not calculate dates further than the year 1999. No one really knows why that is. Maybe whoever created the software never thought we would make it through the millennium - nobody really knows. The problem was solved with a few software packages and millions spent on new hardware. Then the idea of scalability came to fruition. It has been one of the primary ingredients for the survival of companies and software. Can you imagine if Microsoft had to rewrite all of the windows code every time it released a new update?

The moral of this story is simple: Whenever you build anything, especially a program, keep its scalability in mind. What if one million users decide to use your app tomorrow? Is it ready for that? You definitely do not need to build an app for a million people, but you should certainly have the appropriate structure that can support it.

Why Python?

There are many programming languages out there, and there may be more ways to classify them than there are languages. You may have heard of object-oriented programming, or scripting, procedural, etc. This book takes on a very goal-focused approach to things, so we'll classify the languages according to the problem domain or context.

   i. System Languages

  ii. Architectural Languages

  iii. Application Languages

System languages are the best suited to write operating systems, for example, C, C++, or assembler. These languages have been around for a long time and still prove to be useful. Architectural languages are used to build frameworks that make application creation easy. They provide a high level of abstraction, making it easier for the programmer. However, they are slower than the system languages when you run them. A couple of these languages can be C# (C Sharp) or Java. Finally, the application languages are normally used to build the actual business applications. Whenever the company has a web application, like a store or creating different screens for users, they normally have applications that connect with databases and run the features through it. A few examples of this would be Perl, PHP, and ruby.

Python would be considered an application language. However, it does what architectural languages are able to do. Most importantly, the Python syntax - the way the code is written - is much simpler than the other architectural and applications languages.

One of the main reasons Python is a good choice is the fact that the language is easy to read and maintain. Unlike other languages, Python emphasizes on being neat and allows the use of English terms. This readability and clean code approach helps you update and scale the projects you use without going through the syntax nightmares you get with other programming languages.

Python supports different programming paradigms. The features will help you build complex applications. For starters, this language is fully able to integrate oriented and structural programming. There is also plenty of functionality and aspects related to functional and aspect-oriented programming.

Maybe one of the most important reasons that makes Python great is the fact that it is supported by the major systems and platforms. In essence, you can compile your code and run it as is in different platforms, a feature that is the envy of many other languages. It also means that if you, as a programmer, decide to make the change from Windows to mac, Linux or vice versa, you don't have to worry too much about adapting.

Even though this language is considered young, the libraries available are immense and robust. Especially when using modules, you will realize that many of the available ones in the library do most of your code for you. From web applications to operating system interfaces, Python is the place to go. The modules you can download can be very specific to data analysis or neural networking.

Another one of our favorites is the fact that it is open source and comes with a variety of tools and IDEs that are there for free. You can pick and choose the compiler you want along with the modules without having to pay a dime.

So, let's buckle up and get started. Today you join the world of wizardly powers using nothing but a computer and this book.

Chapter 1

Installing Python

One of the first things we need to do is install Python on the computer. There are a few ways to install Python. However, today we will be installing it on the same computer you will be using for coding. Just follow the instructions according to the Operating System you are using on your computer.

To get Python, you should download it from the official Python Software Foundation website that's http://www.Python.org/downloads/. You will find many versions available for download. We will be using version 3.7.4, and it is recommended to use the same version while following this course. Choose either the 32-bit or 64-bit installer according to your Operating System architecture.

Installing Python on Windows

Step 1: Once you have launched the installer, you will see two options. Select the "Install Now" Option.

Step 2: Wait for the launcher to finish the installation process.

Step 3: Next, click on the "Disable path length limit option" and click "Yes" when prompted. This is an outdated restriction that can be easily modified. With that out of the way, it is safe to click on close.

Step 4: Given that we have Python installed, now we need to install a code editor to write the code. There are many editors and IDEs out there. Check the Editor/IDE Matrix to see the different options available.

Installing Python on macOS

Step 1: Getting and installing MacPython

Mac OS X 10.8 comes with Python 2.7 pre-installed by Apple. Regardless, to get the most out of this book, it is essential that you follow the instructions to install Python 3.7. Start by visiting "http://www.Python.org/downloads/mac-osx/ ", then click on the link under the label Python 3.7.4 with the 64-bit/32bit installer.

Step 2: Run the Python installer

A window will appear with information about Python, as shown in the figure below. Click on "Continue" and you're done!

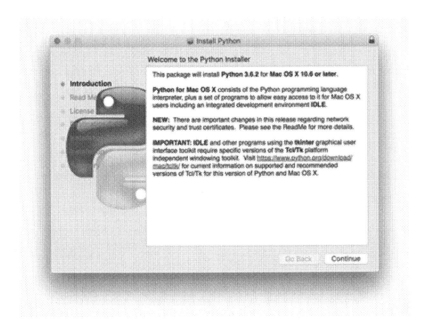

Installing Python on Linux

The following steps are appropriate to install Python on the Ubuntu and LinuxMint operating systems.

Step 1: Prerequisites

Use the commands below to install all the prerequisites for Python.

```
$ sudo apt-get install build-essential checkinstall
$ sudo apt-get install libreadline-gplv2-dev libncursesw5-dev libssl-dev \
libsqlite3-dev tk-dev libgdbm-dev libc6-dev libbz2-dev libffi-dev zlib1g-
dev
```

Step 2: Download Python 3.7

Use these commands to download Python from the official site.

```
$ sudo apt-get install build-essential checkinstall
$ sudo apt-get install libreadline-gplv2-dev libncursesw5-dev libssl-dev \
libsqlite3-dev tk-dev libgdbm-dev libc6-dev libbz2-dev libffi-dev zlib1g-
dev
```

Now extract the downloaded package.

```
$ sudo tar xzf Python-3.7.4.tgz
```

Step 3: Compile Python Source

Run the sets of commands below to compile the Python source code on your system using "altinstall". This is used to prevent the operating system from replacing the default Python binary file.

```
$ cd Python-3.7.4
$ sudo ./configure --enable-optimizations
$ sudo make altinstall
```

Step 4: Check Python Version

To check that the appropriate version has been installed, run the command below.

```
$ Python3.7 -V

Python-3.7.4
```

Installing an Editor /IDE

Now we need to install a code editor / IDE, to interpret the commands that we will need to execute. IDE for the purposes of this book, stands for Integrated Development Environment. Any editor should have the same outcome. In this tutorial, we will be using JetBrains PyCharm. The editor can be downloaded via this link "https://www.jetbrains.com/pycharm/download/".

System Requirements

Requirement	Minimum	Recommended
RAM	4 GB of free RAM	8GB of total system RAM
Disk space	2.5 GB and another 1GB for caches	SSD drive with at least 5 GB of free space
Monitor resolution	1024 x 768	1920 x 1080

	Officially released 64-bit versions of the following: • Microsoft Windows 7 SP1 or later. • macOS 10.11 or later. • Any Linux distribution that supports Gnome, KDE or Unity DE. Pre-release versions are not supported.	Latest 64-bit version of Windows, macOS, or Linux.
Operating system		

Installing PyCharm for Windows

Step 1: Download Pycharm

Visit the JetBrains website and download PyCharm for Windows or use the following link

"https://www.jetbrains.com/pycharm/download/#section=windows".

You will find two versions. To kick-off, you can use the community version as it is both free and an open source.

Step 2: Run the wizard

During the installation process, you will be asked to choose a few options. Mind the following options in the installation wizard. Click on next twice.

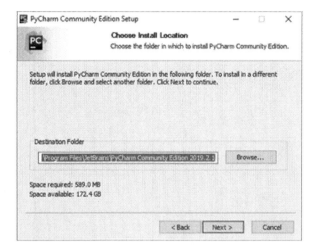

Step 3: Choose your settings

Check the following options, as shown in the image below.

- Create Desktop Shortcut: 64-bit launcher

- Create associations: .py

Now click on next.

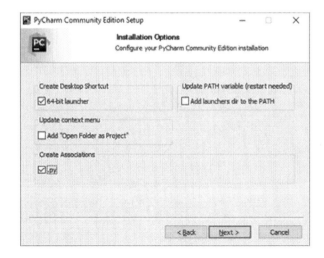

Step 4: Install

Now that all of our settings are ready, click on the install icon and wait for the package to end, then click on 'finish'.

Installing PyCharm on macOS

Step 1: Download Pycharm

Visit the JetBrains website and download PyCharm for macOS or use the following link

"https://www.jetbrains.com/pycharm/download/#section=mac".

You will find two versions. To kick-off you can use the community version as it is both free and an open-source.

Step 2: Mount image

Drag the PyCharm app to the "Applications" folder.

Step 3: Run the image

Start by selecting to not import any settings or select a previous version if you have used PyCharm before.

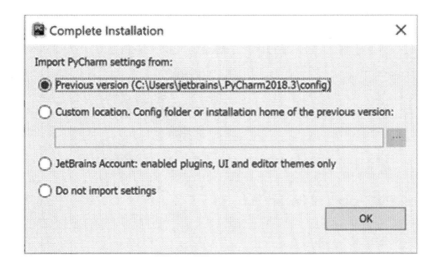

Step 4: User interface

This is how the code editor (IDE) will look. It depends completely on the look and feel that you want. There are two themes available, the Dracula or Light theme, with a black background and a white one respectively.

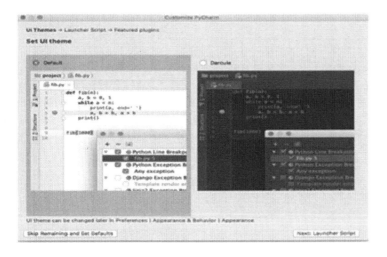

Step 5: In this step, you will be asked to set a path where the script will be created. Just click on next.

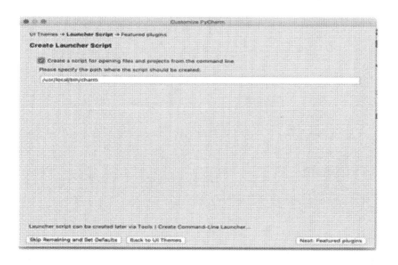

Step 6: Finalizing

Finally, click on start using Pycharm.

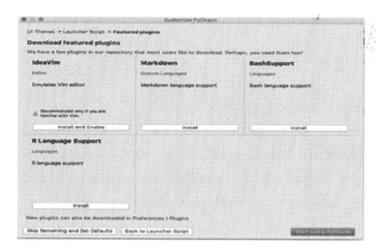

Installing PyCharm on Linux

Most Linux Distros, assuming that it meets the minimum requirements, involve downloading a zipped archive then unpacking it into the "/opt" directory.

Step 1: Download PyCharm from the JetBrains website. Select a local folder for the archive file wherein you can execute the tar command. Download the community version as it is both free and open-sourced.

Step 2: Install PyCharm

Run the following command in a terminal.

```
sudo tar xfz pycharm-*.tar.gz -C /opt/
```

Step 3: Run pycharm.sh from the bin subdirectory

```
cd /opt/pycharm-*/bin
./pycharm.sh
```

Step 4: First time Wizard

Complete the first time run wizard to get started

Editor/ IDE Matrix

Now is the time to introduce something called "IDE", which is short for Integrated Development Environment. IDE is, in essence, a software package that is used to develop and test the software you created. This software package helps automate the task of a developer by reducing the manual effort and combining the most commonly used framework. On the other hand, some developers also prefer Code editors, which is basically a text editor where a developer can write the code used in developing any software. Most importantly, code editors allow the developer to save small text files with the source code instead of the whole project.

IDE	User Rating	Developed in
1. PyCharm	4.5 / 5	Java, Python
2. Spyder	4 / 5	Python
3. PyDev	4.6 / 5	Java, Python
4. Idle	4.2 / 5	Python
5. Wing	4 / 5	C, C++, Python

Chapter 2

Using your Editor /IDE

This section will walk you through the graphical user interface of the IDE that you will be using 'PyCharm'. Most IDEs will have a similar setup with practically the same functionality. However, there are a few code editors that also act as a development platform. There is no shortage of options when it comes to IDEs. Some of the best rated are found in the section above called Editor/ IDE Matrix.

Interface

After installing PyCharm the interface should look similar to the image below. It is divided into three main sections. The first which can be found on the left of the User Interface (UI) is the project tool window where you can store different files for your project. On its right, you should find the Editor that allows you to comfortably type in your code. The editor is packed with automatic indenting, among other features that we will explore throughout this book. Below both panes, we can find the Run Tool Window which executes the output of the code that the programmer decides to run. There are more sections in the user interface. However, these three are the main ones that you should know for now.

- Project tool window,

- Editor,

- Run tool window.

There are a few other sections in the UI that you should be aware of as well for now.

- The navigation bar,

- Status bar.

Creating a Python File

Now that you are familiar with the UI we can create our first Python file. To do that, follow the instructions below:

i. Right click on your folder on the 'Project tool window'.

ii. Select the label called 'New'.

iii. Select 'Python File.'

iv. Type in any file name (preferably without spaces or special characters).

v. Click on enter.

Running code

As part of the programming tradition, the first program a new coder has to make is the 'Hello, world' program. This started when C language was first being created in the Bell labs decades ago. In any case, it is considered to be an initiation of sorts, as it is simple and also allows new coders to test their IDE and be sure it works properly.

In the editor, type in this line of code.

1. **print**('Hello, world')

After writing the line of code, press on the green play button on the top right corner of the editor. Your result should be visible in the run tool window.

Congratulations, you have just written your first program! Although it may not seem like much, this is definitely a milestone along the programming path. The output of your new program can be shown below.

Program output

```
C:\Users\...\PycharmProjects\GettingStarted\venv\Scripts\Python.exe
C:/Users/.../PycharmProjects/GettingStarted/GettingStarted.py
HelloWorld

Process finished with exit code 0
```

Chapter 3

Python Basics

Everyone needs to start somewhere, and this section explores the bare basics that any programmer needs to know to be able to write code. Expect to run into errors as it is part of the learning process. If the IDE gives you an error, just go to your favorite search engine and paste the error message there. By using expressions that are predefined in Python, the computer will interpret the action you want to create and present a result. To write a program is to breakdown big goals into smaller objectives. Most programming initiation starts with sequential programming.

Expressions

This means that the code you write will go from line to line in sequence. The most basic kind of programming instruction in Python is called an Expression. This entails using values and operators to simplify it into a single value just like a calculator. As an example, if we type the code 40 + 2 we would expect Python to return the value of 42.

1. 40 + 2

Most people assume that programmers are good at math. In reality, programmers are mostly writing instructions in a logical way.

Inevitably, a coder is deemed to use math. Below you will find a table on how to use operators for the expressions that you type.

The order of operation is exactly the same as in math. The table below represents the order of precedence from top to bottom. At any point, that can be overridden by using parentheses.

Operator	Operation	Example
**	Exponent	45 ** 3
*	Multiplication	5 * 4
/	Division	4 / 8
//	Integer division	33 // 8
%	Remainder/ modulus	61 % 8
+	Addition	16 + 16
-	Subtraction	19 − 6

Basic Variables

Any seasoned programmer will agree on two facts about coding; 1) Different algorithms can be developed to solve the same problem; 2) Different code can be written to implement the same algorithm. In other words, there are many ways of solving the same problem.

Variable definition

Variables in programming are based on the variables in arithmetic calculations. Think about them as drinking cups that can be filled with different tasty beverages. Sometimes, we will need to predetermine the kind of cup based on what it is we are drinking. Although it can be done, it is not wise to drink hot coffee in a plastic cup. When defining variables, it is essential to tell your IDE what kind it is so that it will deal with it appropriately.

When we refer to variables in programming, we say that they are used to store data to be referenced and used by programs. Moreover, it is good practice to label them with descriptive names, so our programs can be understood clearly. Remember that their sole purpose is to store data in memory.

This is one of the most challenging tasks in computer programming. Many novice programmers struggle with finding names that are meaningful and non-repetitive. Try to always keep in mind that someone else may read your code, so it needs to make sense. That person may as well be your future self, looking for a piece of code that you wrote a few months or maybe years ago.

Naming variables

Names are case sensitive, so if in the same code you have tire, Tire, TiRe, and TIRE, these would be four independent variables in the program. It is becoming more common to use what is called 'camelcase' for variable names. So instead of variables Looking_like_this they lookLikeThis. Note that the Official Python code style, PEP 8, does state that underscores should be used. Regardless, the camelcase is easier to type and elegant.

Whichever method you chose to use, just remember to stick to a certain style throughout your program. If you are going to work as a team on a single program, this is one of the first things you should agree on.

When you assign a variable, remember these important rules:

a. It can only be a single word.

b. It can only have letters, numbers and the underscore character "_".

c. It cannot begin with a number.

Look at the table below to find different acceptable and unacceptable names for variables.

Acceptable variable names	Unacceptable variable names
tire	winter-tire (hyphens are not allowed)
winterTire	winter tire (spaces are not allowed)
winter_tire	8tire (should not begin with a number)
_tire	42 (should not begin with a number)
TIRE	tire_pr!ce (cannot have special characters)
tire3	"tire" (cannot have special characters)

Data Types

Earlier in this section, an analogy of cups was used to represent variables. Imagine that instead of refreshing beverages, you would like to store a radioactive liquid in the cup. This cup should have properties and ways that allow you to deal with it that are different from the ordinary coffee cup.

Each data type has specific characteristics that enable Python to use it accordingly. For instance, an integer can be used in arithmetic operations. However, the mathematic operations are different if the values have decimal points. This is the main reason why most programming languages categorize their data.

The most common data types used in any programming language are:

- Integers,
- Floating-point numbers, and,
- Strings

The table below gives examples of these data types.

Data type	Examples
Integers	-4, -3, -2, -1, 0, 1, 2, 3, 4
Floating-point numbers	-4.25, -4.15, 3.45, 3.14, -1.00
Strings	'a', 'b', 'result', '9 Dogs', 'etc... '

Remember that both integers and floats can be saved as strings. The downside is that you cannot perform any arithmetic operations as long as they are set as a string data type. To put things in perspective, a string is basically the ASCII character codes for the characters between quotations.

That results in the distinction in the binary representation of numbers. For example, the actual number 9 and the ASCII code for the number nine are different in binary. Moreover, a programmer can have a blank string, which is a string without any characters. It is normally used as placeholders for inputs that the user should add in the future. If at any point while programming you see the error *'SyntaxError: EOL while scanning string literal', it is extremely likely that you forgot to close the quote at the end of your string.*

String Data Type

One of the most interesting data types to use when you first start programming must be the string. Human brains are accustomed to see patterns and fill out the blanks. When programming at this level, that is not the case.

String Concatenation is the method of using operators with strings. Once the addition sign between two strings is used, the result will be the first string followed by the other.

In the following example, you will use the print function that is built into Python, and it will display what you want to print on the display. Any function can be called by adding parenthesis after the function name as follows: *print ()*. You can place a string you need to add either quotations or double quotations around the string.

1. **print**('Hello' + 'World') #Displaying two sets of string

2. **#(You can use hashtags to leave comments and notes)**

The value that will be produced will be as follows.

```
C:\Users\...\PycharmProjects\GettingStarted\venv\Scripts\Python.exe
C:/Users/.../PycharmProjects/GettingStarted/Start.py
HelloWorld

Process finished with exit code 0
```

Have you noticed that there is no space between the two words? To add a space character, use one of these methods; 1) Add a space at the end of your first string; 2) Add a space at the beginning of the second string; 3) Add the space character as an independent string between both of the original strings.

1. **print**('Hello'+'World')

2. **print**('Hello '+ 'World')

3. **print**('Hello' + ' World')

4. **print**('Hello' + ' ' + 'World')

The outcome of this program will be as follows.

```
C:\Users\...\PycharmProjects\GettingStarted\venv\Scripts\Python.exe
C:/Users/.../PycharmProjects/GettingStarted/Start.py
HelloWorld
Hello World
Hello World
Hello World

Process finished with exit code 0
```

Another thing that you may notice is that Python cannot concatenate string data with numerical data. The multiplying operator can be used while using string data as it will type the string the number of times you multiply it.

1. **print**('Hello World ' * 5)

The output is shown below.

```
C:\Users\...\PycharmProjects\GettingStarted\venv\Scripts\Python.exe
C:/Users/.../PycharmProjects/GettingStarted/Start.py
Hello World Hello World Hello World Hello World Hello World

Process finished with exit code 0
```

Most programs require some kind of input to be able to process and create useful information. This is where another built-in function in Python is introduced: the "input" function. The user of your program

31

will be prompted with a question that requires an answer before carrying on with the next line of code. Note that the user input in PyCharm is in the output screen, so type the answer there.

1. name = input("What is your name? ") #Note the space after the question mark.

2. **print**('Hi ' + name) #We are concatenating this string.

The output of the interpreter will be:

```
C:\Users\...\PycharmProjects\GettingStarted\venv\Scripts\Python.exe
C:/Users/.../PycharmProjects/GettingStarted/Start.py
What is your name? Indigo
Hi Indigo

Process finished with exit code 0
```

Sometimes it is tricky to use quotation marks with code, especially since printing requires either quotations or double quotations. Let us look at a few examples and see how we can overcome some common problems while using strings.

1. shopName ='Barber shop'

2. shopName2="Barber Shop" #This will give the exact same output

3. **print** (shopName+ ' ---> ' + shopName2)

Program output:

```
C:\Users\...\PycharmProjects\GettingStarted\venv\Scripts\Python.exe
C:/Users/.../PycharmProjects/GettingStarted/Start.py
What is your name? Indigo
Hi Indigo

Process finished with exit code 0
```

In the example above, using double quotations and single quotations did not make a difference. What if the shop is called John's Barber Shop? What if it's called The "Barber shop" with the double quotations in the name?

1. shopName = "John's Barber shop" #An apostrophe in the shop name.

2. shopName2 ='The "Barber Shop"' #Double quotes in the shop name.

3. **print**(shopName + '\n' + shopName2) #Using '\n' will move the following out-put to the next line in the output

Program output:

```
C:\Users\...\PycharmProjects\GettingStarted\venv\Scripts\Python.exe
C:/Users/.../PycharmProjects/GettingStarted/Start.py
John's Barber shop
The "Barber Shop"

Process finished with exit code 0
```

Most coders at some point, need to add a paragraph or a string that needs to be formatted in a certain way with many lines of characters. In cases like these, programmers can use single, double or triple quotations. Just take a look at the following example:

1. msg='''Hello everyone,

2. We are happy to announce a free beer if you pass by on Tuesday's happy hour, between 7:00am and 9:00am.

3. Thank you,

4. Your favorite barber "john".'" #Triple single quotations.

5. msg2= """

6. Hello everyone,

7. We are happy to announce a beer is now available on Tuesday's and Wednesday's Happy Hour, between 7:00am and 9:00am.

8. Thank you,

9. your favorite barber John

10. """ #Triple double quotations.

11. **print**(msg + msg2) #Output of both statements.

Program output:

```
C:\Users\...\PycharmProjects\GettingStarted\venv\Scripts\Python.exe
C:/Users/.../PycharmProjects/GettingStarted/Start.py
Hello everyone,
We are happy to announce a free beer if you pass by on Tuesday's happy
hour, between 7:00am and 9:00am.
Thank you,
Your favorite barber "john".
Hello everyone,
We are happy to announce a beer is now available on Tuesday's and
Wednesday's Happy Hour, between 7:00am and 9:00am.
Thank you,
your favorite barber John

Process finished with exit code 0
```

Finally, programmers using Python can opt to use formatted strings as it is easier to visualize than the regular string concatenation. That is done by simply adding the letter f (lower case) before the quotation, double quotation, or triple quotation. In the case that variables need to be placed within the text, you can use the curly braces to input the variable name. Look at the example below.

1. firstName = "Indigo"

2. lastName = "Montoya"

3. msg1='Hello, my name is ' + firstName + ' ' + lastName + '.You killed my father, prepare to die' #You have to account for spaces

4. **print**(msg1)

5. msg2=f'Hello, my name is {firstName} {lastName}. You killed my father, prepare to die'
   #By using the curly braces you can reserve places for variables.

6. **print**(msg2)

7. msg3=f"'Hello my name is {firstName} {lastName}.

8. You killed my father,

9. prepare to die"'#You can use the formatted string function with triple quotes as well.

Program output

C:\Users\...\PycharmProjects\GettingStarted\venv\Scripts\Python.exe
C:/Users/.../PycharmProjects/GettingStarted/Start.py
Hello, my name is Indigo Montoya. You killed my father, prepare to die
Hello, my name is Indigo Montoya. You killed my father, prepare to die
Hello my name is Indigo Montoya.
You killed my father,
prepare to die

Process finished with exit code 0

There are cases where a programmer needs to format the string provided by the user. These few commands (methods) will surely come in handy once you start getting massive amounts of data. To call a method, you need to type the name of the variable, followed by a period, then followed by the method.

1. msg = input('What say you? ')

2. **print**(msg) #Original message

3. **print**(msg.upper()) #All Caps

4. **print**(msg.lower()) #All small

5. **print**(msg.title()) #Title case

Program output:

```
C:\Users\...\PycharmProjects\GettingStarted\venv\Scripts\Python.exe
C:/Users/.../PycharmProjects/GettingStarted/Start.py
What say you? Save the rainforrest
Save the rainforrest
SAVE THE RAINFORREST
save the rainforrest
Save The Rainforrest

Process finished with exit code 0
```

Sometimes programmers need to extract certain characters from a string, or find out how long a string of data is. To extract a certain character a programmer needs to know the index of all the characters. To get started, we should find out what the length of a string is.

1. msg = input('What say you? ')

2. **print**(msg) #Original message

3. **print** (len(msg)) #Built-
    in function to know the length of a message

Program output:

```
C:\Users\...\PycharmProjects\GettingStarted\venv\Scripts\Python.exe
C:/Users/.../PycharmProjects/GettingStarted/Start.py
What say you? Help me, please
Help me, please
14

Process finished with exit code 0
```

The table below represents a string and its index.

H	e	l	p		m	e	,		p	l	e	a	s	e
0	1	2	3	4	5	6	7	8	9	10	11	12	13	14

One of the benefits of using Python is that you can use a negative index. For instance, you decide to extract a character of a string that is closer to the end. The programmer may not be aware of what the length of the string is in this case. However, he knows that he needs to extract a character from right to left.

H	e	l	p		m	e	,		p	l	e	a	s	e
...	-14	-13	-12	-11	-10	-9	-8	-7	-6	-5	-4	-3	-2	-1

The next few lines of code will explain how to extract specific characters from a string. Indexing allows a programmer to extract specific characters like the first last or character *n* with ease. Another option is to use a range of characters by adding two parameters indicating the beginning and end of the characters being indexed. If the code does not explicitly state what the first indexed character should be in a range, it will always assume it's the first. If the program does not state where to stop in the end parameter, the interpreter will assume that it is the last character in the string.

1. name= input("What's your name? ")

2. **print**(name[0]) #This will print the first character.

3. **print**(name[-1]) #This will print the last character.

4. **print**(name[0:4]) #This will print the first four characters.

5. **print** (name[4:])

   #Will print starting from the fourth character to the last one.

6. **print** (name[:9])

   #Will print starting from the first character to the ninth.

7. **print**(name[1:-1]) #This will exclude the first and last letters.

Program output:

```
C:\Users\...\PycharmProjects\GettingStarted\venv\Scripts\Python.exe
C:/Users/.../PycharmProjects/GettingStarted/Start.py
What's your name? John Smith
J
h
John
Smith
John Smit
ohn Smit

Process finished with exit code 0
```

Integer Type

One of the best things about Python is that integers do not really have any programmable cap to how long they can be. The only realistic constraint found is how much memory you have on the computer executing your program.

1. x = 100000000000000000000 *12344567890

2. **print**(x)

39

Program output:

```
C:\Users\...\PycharmProjects\GettingStarted\venv\Scripts\Python.exe
C:/Users/.../PycharmProjects/GettingStarted/Start.py
1234456789000000000000000000000000

Process finished with exit code 0
```

Python assumes that the programmer will be using a decimal number system by default and does not require a prefix to use it. A decimal number system is a system that you use to represent numbers, by utilizing digits from 0 to 9 and rolling over after. So, in essence, we add another digit after we reach 9 to the left and start counting again. There are other number systems, the most famous being the binary which is used by computers and hexadecimal as it makes it easier to understand binary.

If a programmer decides to use a different number system, also known as base-number, they can use the prefixes in the table below.

Prefix	Base	Interpretation
0b (zero + lowercase letter 'b') 0B (zero + uppercase letter 'B')	2	Binary
0o (zero + lowercase letter 'o') 0O (zero + uppercase letter 'O')	8	Octal
0x (zero + lowercase letter 'x') 0X (zero + uppercase letter 'X')	16	Hexadecimal

To try it out, you can ask Python to print out the decimal values of different number base representation.

1. **print**(10) #Base 10 (decimal).

2. **print**(0o10) #Base 8 (octal).

3. **print**(0x100) #Base 16 (hexadecimal).

4. **print**(0b10) #Base 2 (binary).

Program output:

```
C:\Users\...\PycharmProjects\GettingStarted\venv\Scripts\Python.exe
C:/Users/.../PycharmProjects/GettingStarted/Start.py
10
8
256
2

Process finished with exit code 0
```

Floats type

The floating-point data type is a numerical type based on the decimal system that allows the variables to have decimal points. There is a built-in automatic function where Python will change an integer to a floating-point in the case that it requires to, such as in dividing numbers.

1. x = 8 / 7 # Dividing 8 by 7

2. **print**(x)

3. y = 8 / 4 # Dividing 8 by 4

41

4. **print**(y)

5. z = 8 // 4 # Dividing 8 by four but only retrieving an integer.

6. **print**(z)

Program output:

```
C:\Users\...\PycharmProjects\GettingStarted\venv\Scripts\Python.exe
C:/Users/.../PycharmProjects/GettingStarted/Start.py
1.1428571428571428
2.0
2

Process finished with exit code 0
```

A programmer can incorporate floating values with other mathematical functions. Spend a few minutes going through the documentation found in this link,

(https://docs.Python.org/3/tutorial/introduction.html#numbers) if the coding you are going to use is math-intensive.

Converting data types

At the beginning of programming, when to use certain data types can be confusing. In many cases, the data that a programmer needs to use is not really up to them. Data conversion can be a life savior while writing code. Here are a few examples of data conversion and how to identify the data type of a variable.

1. example = 20

2. example=int(example) # Changing the type to an integer.

3. **print**(type(example)) #
   This shows the type of variable you have.

4. example = str(example) # Changing into a string.

5. **print**(type(example)) #
   This shows the type of variable you have.

6. example = float(example) # Changing into a floating-point.

7. **print**(type(example)) #
   This shows the type of variable you have.

8. example=False

9. example = bool(example) # Changing into a boolean.

10. **print**(type(example)) #
    This shows the type of variable you have.

Program output:

```
C:\Users\...\PycharmProjects\GettingStarted\venv\Scripts\Python.exe
C:/Users/.../PycharmProjects/GettingStarted/Start.py
<class 'int'>
<class 'str'>
<class 'float'>
<class 'bool'>

Process finished with exit code 0
```

Assigning a Value to Variables

This involves initializing a variable the first time a value is stored. In this example, we are placing the price of tires. While verbalizing, the best thing to do is to state the following command as 'Putting forty into tires' because the equal sign, as we will learn later, is also used to compare variables.

1. tire = 40

2. **print**(tire)

Program output:

The output for this declaration is 40, so the program will display 40.

```
C:\Users\...\PycharmProjects\GettingStarted\venv\Scripts\Python.exe
C:/Users/.../PycharmProjects/GettingStarted/Start.py
40

Process finished with exit code 0
```

Now, let's try to add taxes to the price of the tires. If you assign a new value to a variable that has already been initiated, the old value is erased. Seriously. Gone. Not coming back. Unless you re-run the program.

Let's look at an example below.

1. tire = 40

2. taxes= 2

3. taxedTire =tire + taxes

4. **print**(taxedTire)

Program output:

In this case, we initiated the price of tires to 40 and the cost of taxes to 2. Then we changed the tire cost to be equal to the initial value (40) plus the price of taxes (2) which gives us an output of 42.

```
C:\Users\...\PycharmProjects\GettingStarted\venv\Scripts\Python.exe
C:/Users/.../PycharmProjects/GettingStarted/Start.py
42

Process finished with exit code 0
```

In this next example we will copy the value of a variable to another variable, by using the same example above.

1. tire = 40

2. taxes= 2

3. taxedTire =tire + taxes

4. tire = taxedTire

5. **print**(tire)

Program output:

```
C:\Users\...\PycharmProjects\GettingStarted\venv\Scripts\Python.exe
C:/Users/.../PycharmProjects/GettingStarted/Start.py
42

Process finished with exit code 0
```

Just as we assigned numbers to the variables, you can also initialize a variable with a string. To let Python know that you want to store a string and not another variable, we need to use quotation marks.

1. tireOrigin = 'Japan'

2. **print**(tireOrigin)

Program output:

```
C:\Users\...\PycharmProjects\GettingStarted\venv\Scripts\Python.exe
C:/Users/.../PycharmProjects/GettingStarted/Start.py
Japan

Process finished with exit code 0
```

For this next example, we will want to display the price and the place it was made as an output. By adding the plus sign between words, it will display both strings side by side.

1. tireOrigin = 'Japan'

2. tirePrice = 42

3. tireOutput = tireOrigin + str(tirePrice)

4. **print**(tireOutput)

Program output:

```
C:\Users\...\PycharmProjects\GettingStarted\venv\Scripts\Python.exe
C:/Users/.../PycharmProjects/GettingStarted/Start.py
Japan42

Process finished with exit code 0
```

At this point, it would make sense to add a space character in between Japan and 42. Now that's what a space is: A character! Once you place an addition symbol followed by the space character between quotations, then place another addition symbol followed by the second variable. Look at the code below.

1. tireOrigin = 'Japan'

2. tirePrice = 42

3. tireOutput = tireOrigin + ' ' + str(tirePrice)

4. **print**(tireOutput)

Program output:

```
C:\Users\...\PycharmProjects\GettingStarted\venv\Scripts\Python.exe
C:/Users/.../PycharmProjects/GettingStarted/Start.py
Japan 42

Process finished with exit code 0
```

Arithmetic Operations

To start using mathematical operations, you need to know that it is as simple as using a calculator. There is not much more to it. Try a few arithmetic operations of your own, or see the results of the operations below.

1. number = 5 + 6 * 7 / 4.0

2. **print**(number)

3. remainder = 8 % 5

4. **print**(remainder)

5. squared = 177 ** 2

6. cubed = 3 ** 3

7. **print**(squared)

8. **print**(cubed)

9. intergerDivision = 8 // 3

10. **print**(integerDivision)

Program output:

```
C:\Users\...\PycharmProjects\GettingStarted\venv\Scripts\Python.exe
C:/Users/.../PycharmProjects/GettingStarted/Start.py
15.5
3
31329
27

Process finished with exit code 0
```

A useful operation that is constantly used during programming is called an augmented assignment operator. This operation is used when the programmer needs to increment a certain variable. Look at the examples below.

1. x = 10

2. x =x + 6 #This will take the original value of x and add six to it.

3. **print**(x)

4. y = 10

5. y += 6 #This will also add 6 to y.

6. **print**(y)

7. z=10

8. z -= 6 #This will subtract 6 from the original value of z

9. **print**(z)

10. q = 10

11. q *= 6 #This will multiply the original value of q by 6

12. **print**(q)

Program output:

```
C:\Users\...\PycharmProjects\GettingStarted\venv\Scripts\Python.exe
C:/Users/.../PycharmProjects/GettingStarted/Start.py
16
16
4
60

Process finished with exit code 0
```

As a bonus, here are a couple of useful built-in functions that can be used according to the programmer's needs. In some cases, a coder may find the need to round up numbers or use absolute numbers. An absolute number is the positive version of the number regardless of the outcome. Type in the few lines of code that follow and see them in action.

1. x = 3.1415926 #This is pi to the seventh digit.

2. **print**(x)

3. **print**(round(x)) #By rounding x, the outcome should be an integer

4. y = -9343

5. **print**(y)

6. **print**(abs(y)) #By setting it as an absolute number, the output will be positive.

Program output:

```
C:\Users\...\PycharmProjects\GettingStarted\venv\Scripts\Python.exe
C:/Users/.../PycharmProjects/GettingStarted/Start.py
3.1415926
3
-9343
9343

Process finished with exit code 0
```

Math functions

Python has a math module that provides most of the common mathematical functions. Just like conventional arithmetic operations, this module will operate using the same basic principles. A module is a collection of functions placed in a file. Before being able to use a module, you need to import it in your code. To import the math module, all you need to do is enter the command below.

1. **import** math

In order to call a function from a module that has been imported, a dot notation has to be used. If a programmer needs to call the log function, they would start with the module name followed by the function name. The example below shows a dot notation in lines three and four while calling for the pi and sin functions, respectively.

1. **import** math #Here we are importing the math module (file).

2. degrees = 90

3. angle = degrees * 2 * math.*pi* / 360.0 #On this method we are calling for *pi*.

4. **print**(math.*sin*(angle)) #In this method we are using the *sin* method to calculate an angle.

5. x = 3.8

6. **print**(math.ceil(x)) #Here we are calculating the ceiling of x.

7. **print**(math.floor(x)) #Here we are looking for the floor value of x.

There is a considerable amount of functions that you can use in the math module. Visit the Python library that has all of the functions listed along with examples and explanations

(https://docs.Python.org/3/library/math.html).

Lists

Lists are some of the handiest variables of the different data types programmers use. Most commonly, they are used to write comma-separated files, which are a simple version of spreadsheets. Lists tend to contain the same data type. However, there are cases where you can add different data types in the same list.

1. groceryList =['Apples', 'Oranges', 'Rice', 'Juice', 'Avocado']

2. **print**(groceryList)

Program output:

```
C:\Users\...\PycharmProjects\GettingStarted\venv\Scripts\Python.exe
C:/Users/.../PycharmProjects/GettingStarted/Start.py
['Apples', 'Oranges', 'Rice', 'Juice', 'Avocado']

Process finished with exit code 0
```

Just like strings, lists can be indexed according to their place on the list. Later on in this section we will learn how to alter items in a list variable.

1. groceryList =['Apples', 'Oranges', 'Rice', 'Juice', 'Avocado']

2. **print**(groceryList) # Printing the whole list

3. **print**(groceryList[0]) # Printing the first item on the list

4. **print**(groceryList[-1]) # Printing the last item on the list

Program output:

```
C:\Users\...\PycharmProjects\GettingStarted\venv\Scripts\Python.exe
C:/Users/.../PycharmProjects/GettingStarted/Start.py
['Apples', 'Oranges', 'Rice', 'Juice', 'Avocado']
Apples
Avocado

Process finished with exit code 0
```

To update a list and add new items is as simple as placing an addition operator with the items you want to add after the list variable. If we need to add a few items to our grocery list, we can simply do that as shown below.

1. groceryList =['Apples', 'Oranges', 'Rice', 'Juice', 'Avocado']

2. **print**(groceryList) # Printing the whole list

3. groceryList= groceryList + ['Pasta', 'Pepper', 'Tomatoes']
   #Adding items to the list

4. **print**(groceryList) # Printing updated list

Program output:

```
C:\Users\...\PycharmProjects\GettingStarted\venv\Scripts\Python.exe
C:/Users/.../PycharmProjects/GettingStarted/Start.py
['Apples', 'Oranges', 'Rice', 'Juice', 'Avocado']
['Apples', 'Oranges', 'Rice', 'Juice', 'Avocado', 'Pasta', 'Pepper', 'Tomatoes']

Process finished with exit code 0
```

There are cases where an item of a list needs to be replaced. In that case, we can use the square brackets to change a specific item.

1. groceryList =['Apples', 'Oranges', 'Rice', 'Juice', 'Avocado','Pasta', 'Pepper']

2. **print**(groceryList) # Printing the whole list

3. groceryList[3]= 'Mangoes' #
   Instead of Juice we can replace it with Mangoes

4. **print**(groceryList) # Printing the updated list

Program output:

```
C:\Users\...\PycharmProjects\GettingStarted\venv\Scripts\Python.exe
C:/Users/.../PycharmProjects/GettingStarted/Start.py
['Apples', 'Oranges', 'Rice', 'Juice', 'Avocado', 'Pasta', 'Pepper']
['Apples', 'Oranges', 'Rice', 'Mangoes', 'Avocado', 'Pasta', 'Pepper']

Process finished with exit code 0
```

Another way to add items to a list is using the append method by adding a dot notation with the append method, followed by parenthesis.

1. groceryList =['Apples', 'Oranges', 'Rice', 'Juice', 'Avocado']

2. **print**(groceryList) # Printing the whole list

3. groceryList.append('Strawberries')

4. **print**(groceryList)

Program output

C:\Users\...\PycharmProjects\GettingStarted\venv\Scripts\Python.exe
C:/Users/.../PycharmProjects/GettingStarted/Start.py
['Apples', 'Oranges', 'Rice', 'Juice', 'Avocado']
['Apples', 'Oranges', 'Rice', 'Juice', 'Avocado', 'Strawberries']

Process finished with exit code 0

There are other options to replace items in the list in bulk by using the index. For example, you can replace indices from three to five.

1. groceryList =['Apples', 'Oranges', 'Rice', 'Juice', 'Avocado', 'Bananas']

2. **print**(groceryList) # Printing the whole list

3. groceryList[3:5] = ['Salmon', 'Bacon'] # This only replaces index three and four

4. **print**(groceryList)
   # What if we add an extra item with no real assignment?

5. groceryList[3:5] = ['Grapes', 'Cucumber', 'Olives']
   #Python will append the extra item and move the fifth item to the sixth index

6. **print**(groceryList)

Program output

C:\Users\...\PycharmProjects\GettingStarted\venv\Scripts\Python.exe
C:/Users/.../PycharmProjects/GettingStarted/Start.py
['Apples', 'Oranges', 'Rice', 'Juice', 'Avocado', 'Bananas']
['Apples', 'Oranges', 'Rice', 'Salmon', 'Bacon', 'Bananas']
['Apples', 'Oranges', 'Rice', 'Grapes', 'Cucumber', 'Olives', 'Bananas']

Process finished with exit code 0

Previously, we explored the 'len()' function in both the variables and string data type sections. The built-in function can also be used to know the length of a list variable. In the future, a programmer importing information from a comma-separated file can know how many values are actually there. For the time being, we will use the example we had. Just keep in mind that it will become very useful when dealing with large sums of data.

1. groceryList =['Apples', 'Oranges', 'Rice', 'Juice', 'Avocado', 'Bananas']

2. **print**(len(groceryList)) #
   Printing the length of the list variable

Program output:

C:\Users\...\PycharmProjects\GettingStarted\venv\Scripts\Python.exe
C:/Users/.../PycharmProjects/GettingStarted/Start.py
6

Process finished with exit code 0

In later chapters we will explore how to use lists to store information that is calculated using arithmetic calculations, loops and logic.

List methods

Part of becoming a programmer is finding information about techniques and methods that you need based on the project at hand. Here are a few methods that you can use with lists, simplified in a table. That said, you can always Google specific information. The art of being able to find specific methods or pieces of information falls to the basic understanding and knowledge of the specific terminology in question.

Method	Explanation
groceryList.append(x)	Add a value at the end of the list. On this case it is the value of 'x'.
groceryList.extend([x , y])	Iterates values to the end of the list. You can store multiple list items separately. If this is tried using the append method it will store one value instead of two.
groceryList.insert(1, x)	This will append the value of 'x' in index 1.
groceryList.remove(x)	This will remove the first item from the list with a value equivalent to 'x'.
groceryList.pop( )	This returns and then removes the last item on the list.
groceryList.clear( )	This removes all the items in the list.
groceryList.index(x)	This will return the index value that corresponds with 'x'

groceryList.count(x)	This will return the number of times the corresponding value of 'x' is found on the list.
groceryList.sort(x)	This sorts the list in ascending order.
groceryList.reverse (x)	This reverses the order of the list.
groceryList.copy (x)	This makes a copy of the list.

Tuples

Tuples are a special kind of list, as there is a lot of functionality that does not exist in it. For starters, you cannot add or remove elements in a tuple as it immutable. Tuples still have the capability of searching elements in the list as well as using an 'in' operator for complex logical operations.

Why use tuples at all then? The answer is simple. Its immutability. This particular property makes tuples faster to process than lists, as their overall length is static and not dynamic like its other counterparts. Moreover, tuples can be used as dictionary keys, another data type that will be discussed later in this book. Another good reason is security, as you can write protect your data that does not need to change. Without a doubt, one of the main reasons for its popularity is aesthetical. A lot of functions in Python require braces as well as round brackets, and tuples use square brackets. Square brackets are only used when dealing with lists that make it easier for coders to find data being passed to a function or another variable.

A tuple is a number of variables separated by commas. Take a look at the code example below.

1. thoughts = 'Tesla Model 3', 1969, 3.14 #
   Tuple list can have different data types in it.

2. **print**(thoughts)

3. otherThoughts = thoughts, 'Onion Soup', 'Georgia trip', 911 #
   Nesting tuples

4. **print**(otherThoughts)

5. thoughts[1] = 1991 #
   Tuples are immutable, you cannot change them

6. **print**(thoughts)

Program output:

```
C:\Users\...\PycharmProjects\GettingStarted\venv\Scripts\Python.exe
C:/Users/.../PycharmProjects/GettingStarted/Start.py
 File "C:/Users/
/PycharmProjects/GettingStarted/MyFirstProgram.py", line 5, in
<module>
   thoughts[1] = 1991 # Tuples are immutable, you cannot change them
TypeError: 'tuple' object does not support item assignment
('Tesla Model 3', 1969, 3.14)
(('Tesla Model 3', 1969, 3.14), 'Onion Soup', 'Georgia trip', 911)

Process finished with exit code 1
```

Unpacking tuples

To assign a value to a variable, it requires that the variable be is the left-hand side of an equal sign followed by the actual values on the other side. You can use a tuple to assign multiple variables at the same time. For instance, if you have coded a game and you want to reset all of your values at once, you can use a tuple to reset the score, player name, etc. Another attribute that distinguishes a tuple is that if you want to have only one element in your list, you still need to follow it with a comma so that Python can interpret the variable as a tuple. If the coder wants to create an empty tuple, with no values, the parenthesis needs to be empty.

1. nothing = () # A tuple with an empty value.

2. **print**(nothing)

3. survivalTools =('rope',) #Remember to leave a comma at the end if you only need one value.

4. **print**(survivalTools)

5. reset =(0, 'The Courtyard', 1.99) # Creating a tuple for reset

6. score, levelName, availableCurrency = reset

7. **print**(score, levelName, availableCurrency)

Chapter 4

Dictionaries

In this chapter, we will cover a new data type which facilitates a flexible way to organize data. Using the knowledge in the previous section about lists, soon you will be able to create data structures that will be useful in almost any application you may think of.

A dictionary can store many values just like a list. However, they can index different data types. Keys of a dictionary are associated with values. When combined, that is called the key-value pair. Let's start by creating a new dictionary variable.

1. flat = {'rooms': '2', 'bathrooms': '1', 'floor': '3rd', 'apartment': '306'} # Note the curly braces

2. **print**(f"My Apartment has {flat['rooms']} rooms, {flat['bathrooms']} bathroom")

Program output:

```
C:\Users\...\PycharmProjects\GettingStarted\venv\Scripts\Python.exe
C:/Users/.../PycharmProjects/GettingStarted/Start.py
My Apartment has 2 rooms, 1 bathroom
Process finished with exit code 0
```

Dictionaries, unlike lists, can be identified by other data types that are not necessarily integers, although it can use integers as keys as well.

Dictionaries vs. lists

The order of list items does matter when trying to compare them to other lists. Meanwhile, dictionaries can find if a list that already exists, even if the keys are out of order. This does not mean that the order is not important. If a coder maintains a uniform order in their lists, then this is not an issue. However, the main problem appears once you start getting unordered data, especially from users.

Try this following sequence in the editor.

1. flat = ['rooms', 'bathrooms', 'floor', 'apartment']

2. apartment = ['apartment', 'bathrooms', 'rooms', 'floor']

3. **print**(flat == apartment) #When you use == you are asking if they are equal to each other

4. flat = {'rooms': '2', 'bathrooms': '1', 'floor': '3rd', 'apartment': '306'} # Note the curly braces

5. apartment = {'apartment': '306', 'bathrooms': '1', 'rooms': '2', 'floor': '3rd'}

6. **print**(flat == apartment)

Program output:

```
C:\Users\...\PycharmProjects\GettingStarted\venv\Scripts\Python.exe
C:/..
False
True

Process finished with exit code 0
```

Useful methods

There are a few useful methods that you can use with dictionaries. These methods are particularly useful when combined with loops. All of the following methods need to be used by adding a dot notation after the name of the variable followed by a parenthesis.

The first method is the keys(), which will output the keys to a dictionary. The next method is the value(), which will output the values of keys. The last method is the items() which will output both the keys and values between parenthesis and separated by a comma.

Try out the example below.

1. flat = {'rooms': '2', 'bathrooms': '1', 'floor': '3rd', 'apartment': '306'}

2. **print**(flat.keys())

3. **print**(flat.values())

4. **print**(flat.items())

Program output:

```
C:\Users\...\PycharmProjects\GettingStarted\venv\Scripts\Python.exe
C:/Users/.../PycharmProjects/GettingStarted/MyFirstProgram.py
dict_keys(['rooms', 'bathrooms', 'floor', 'apartment'])
dict_values(['2', '1', '3rd', '306'])
dict_items([('rooms', '2'), ('bathrooms', '1'), ('floor', '3rd'), ('apartment',
'306')])

Process finished with exit code 0
```

Value or key check

While using a dictionary, one of the functions that will most likely be needed regularly is to check for a certain value in your dictionary. For this exercise, we will be using two operators; the 'in' and the 'not' operators. These two operators can tell you if a certain key or value in a dictionary exists. Note that these operators can also be used in lists as well as logic. These operators will come out with a Boolean output either 'True' or 'False'.

Here are some lines of codes to try out.

1. flat = {'rooms': 2, 'bathrooms': 1, 'floor': '3rd', 'apartment': 306}

2. **print**('rooms' **in** flat.keys()) #
   Determining if there is a key called rooms

3. **print**('1st' **in** flat.values()) #
   Determining if there is a value called 1st

4. **print**(3 **not in** flat.items()) #Determining if there is neither a value nor key of 3

Program output:

```
C:\Users\...\PycharmProjects\GettingStarted\venv\Scripts\Python.exe
C:/Users/.../PycharmProjects/GettingStarted/MyFirstProgram.py
True
False
True

Process finished with exit code 0
```

64

There is another method that can be used with dictionaries, and it makes it easy to fetch a specific piece of data. This is called the get() method.

Check out the example below, to see how it is used inside the editor.

1. flat = {'rooms': 2, 'bathrooms': 1, 'floor': '3rd', 'apartment': 306}

2. **print**(f"I live in the apartment {flat.get('apartment')}") #getting the apartment number

Program Output:

```
C:\Users\...\PycharmProjects\GettingStarted\venv\Scripts\Python.exe
C:/Users/.../PycharmProjects/GettingStarted/MyFirstProgram.py
I live in the apartment 306

Process finished with exit code 0
```

Chapter 5

Loops

We have all been in a situation where we're stuck doing the same thing over and over again at work or at home. For the longest time in history, man has been held back by the burden of repeating tasks. Computers will repeat any commands flawlessly, unlike humans who are expected to make mistakes from time to time.

In this chapter, we will learn about another classic of loops programming. Just like the name suggests, loops repeat a block of code until a certain condition is met. In Python, we have three types of loops, and we will be exploring them all in this chapter.

While loops

This particular loop will continue working until a certain condition is met. In this first example, we will use an iteration variable named I to show the even numbers up until it reaches 10.

1. i=0

2. **while** i <=10: #
    Note if you do not add the equal sign, Python will not print the last value of 10

3.   **print** (i) # Printing i to the screen

4.   i+=2 # Adding two on every loop revolution

Do not forget to press on shift+tab to close this block of code.

Program output:

```
C:\Users\...\PycharmProjects\GettingStarted\venv\Scripts\Python.exe
C:/Users/.../PycharmProjects/GettingStarted/MyFirstProgram.py
0
2
4
6
8
10

Process finished with exit code 0
```

Now, just as we used an operator to decide when to stop, this time we'll use the length of a list to stop the loop. In this case, we are going to print the names of everyone on a list along with a welcome message.

1. nameList=['Adam', 'Nathan', 'Joe', 'Mark', 'Jose', 'Jack']

2. **while** nameList:

3.   **print**(f"Welcome {nameList.pop(-1)}, to Johnny's party")

#Pop() method takes the last name of the list, prints it and
then removes it from the list

#Remember to press on shift+tab to close this code block

Program output:

```
C:\Users\...\PycharmProjects\GettingStarted\venv\Scripts\Python.exe
C:/Users/.../PycharmProjects/GettingStarted/MyFirstProgram.py
Welcome Jack, to Johnny's party
Welcome Jose, to Johnny's party
Welcome Mark, to Johnny's party
Welcome Joe, to Johnny's party
Welcome Nathan, to Johnny's party
Welcome Adam, to Johnny's party

Process finished with exit code 0
```

If you do not like to use the pop method while utilizing lists, you can use the length of a list in your loop. Some programmers prefer not to use the pop method, as it removes values from the list that may be needed in the future. Look at the example below that accomplishes that without losing any item from the list.

1. nameList=['Adam', 'Nathan', 'Joe', 'Mark', 'Jose', 'Jack'] # List variable with all names.

2. x = 0 # Initial value for loop break.

3. **while** x < len(nameList): # While x is smaller than the length of the list.

4. **print**(f"Welcome {nameList[x]}, to Johnny's party") # Printing the welcome message.

5. x += 1 # Iterating one to x on every cycle.

Program output:

Another method of stopping a loop is using a break command. In the example below, the program is trying to identify the closest number to 1000 that is divisible by 14.

1. i = 1000 # The initil value of i

2. **while** i >= 0: #

   This will keep the loop running until i is equal to zero.

3.   **if** i % 14 ==0: #

   If the remainder of the division by 14 is to zero.

4.   **print**(i) # Printing the required value.

5.   **break** # Stop (break) the program.

6.   i-=1 # Subtracting one on each revolution of the loop

Program output:

In this next example for while loops, we will be creating a program that will prompt for a password. After three times, if the password is not correct, it will send a message to the user asking them to try again later. However, if the password is correct, the program will display a success message.

1. pwd1 = "password" #The password that is saved in the program

2. i = 0

3. pwdPass = False

4. **while** i < 3: # This will give the user three attempts

5.   userPwd = input(f"Please insert the password: ")
#Daving user password into a variable.

6.   i += 1 # Incrementing i to break the loop after three attempts.

7.   **if** pwd1 == userPwd:
#Checking saved password with the user password.

8.   pwdMsg = "You're pure of heart, you may pass."

9.   **break** # Breaking the loop as there is no need to run it again.

10. **else**: # Kust like an if statement you can have an
else statement in a while loop

11.   pwdMsg = "You're unworthy, only the pure of heart may pass!"

12. **print**(pwdMsg) # Printing the message after the loop is finished.

Program output:

```
C:\Users\...\PycharmProjects\GettingStarted\venv\Scripts\Python.exe
C:/Users/.../PycharmProjects/GettingStarted/MyFirstProgram.py
Please insert the password: Password
Please insert the password: PASSWORD
Please insert the password: password
You're pure of heart, you may pass.

Process finished with exit code 0
```

Finally, we are going to create an old school simple game using a while loop. In this game, the user will decide if he wants to start or stop a toy train, with the option of quitting. Let's take a look at the code.

1. userCommand = '' #
    Creating an empty variable to store the user command.

2. **while** True: #
    This will keep the loop going until it is broken inside the loop

3. userCommand = input('>>> ') #
    We use this to give the program a retro look.

4. **if** userCommand.lower() == 'start':

5. #
    Note the lower case method, this is to avoid lower or upper case prob
    lems with the user.

6. **print**('train has started')

7. **elif** userCommand.lower() == 'stop':

8. **print**('train has stopped')

9. **elif** userCommand.lower() == 'quit':

10. **print**('See you later...')

11.   **break** # This will break the program if the user wants to quit.

12.   **elif** userCommand.lower() == 'help':

13.   **print(f"""**

14.   Start ===> To start the train

15.   Stop ===> To stop the train

16.   Quit ===> To exit program """)

17.   **else**:

18.   **print(**

19.   "Sorry, I can't understand you. type Help for assistance.") # This is displayed so that the user knows what the options are.

Program output:

```
C:\Users\...\PycharmProjects\GettingStarted\venv\Scripts\Python.exe
C:/Users/.../PycharmProjects/GettingStarted/MyFirstProgram.py
>>> Start train
Sorry, I can't understand you. type Help for assistance.
>>> HELP

    Start ===> To start the train
    Stop ===> To stop the train
    Quit ===> To exit program
>>> Start
train has started
>>> stop
train has stopped
>>> Quit
See you later...


Process finished with exit code 0
```

For loops

A 'for loop' is normally used when you know how many times you are going to loop exactly. In the case where you can break spontaneously, you should use a while loop. Moreover, 'for loops' are very useful with strings. The first example will show you how Python can iterate a string.

1. **for** item **in** 'Roger': # This is the condition of the for loop

2.   **print**(item)

Program output:

```
C:\Users\...\PycharmProjects\GettingStarted\venv\Scripts\Python.exe
C:/Users/.../PycharmProjects/GettingStarted/MyFirstProgram.py
R
o
g
e
r

Process finished with exit code 0
```

Remember the exercise we did when printing out the names on a list? It is a breeze in comparison when using a 'for loop'. Let's check it out.

1. nameList = ['Adam', 'Nathan', 'Joe', 'Mark', 'Jose', 'Jack'] # Initial list of names

2. **for** item **in** nameList: # This will run every item of the list.

3.   **print**(item) # This will print every item on the list.

Do not forget to use shift and tab to close the block of code.

Program output:

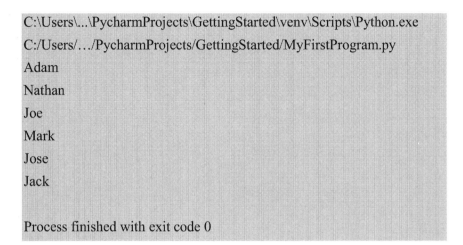

```
C:\Users\...\PycharmProjects\GettingStarted\venv\Scripts\Python.exe
C:/Users/.../PycharmProjects/GettingStarted/MyFirstProgram.py
Adam
Nathan
Joe
Mark
Jose
Jack

Process finished with exit code 0
```

There is a built-in function that can be used with the 'for loop' called the range function. This can be used to print out a range of numbers starting from zero.

1. **for** item **in** range(5): #
   This range will give us an output from zero to four

2. **print**(item)

Program output:

```
C:\Users\...\PycharmProjects\GettingStarted\venv\Scripts\Python.exe
C:/Users/.../PycharmProjects/GettingStarted/MyFirstProgram.py
0
1
2
3
4

Process finished with exit code 0
```

The range function has the option to select a specific range – for example, from 5 to 12. It can also specify the steps. That means if you want to iterate it every time by two, you can add a third parameter to do that. Let's look at an example.

1. **for** item **in** range(5, 25, 5): #
   First parameter start range, second parameter end range, third parameter steps

2.   **print**(item)

Program output:

```
C:\Users\...\PycharmProjects\GettingStarted\venv\Scripts\Python.exe
C:/Users/.../PycharmProjects/GettingStarted/MyFirstProgram.py
5
10
15
20

Process finished with exit code 0
```

Now for this last example, let's imagine that you want to add all of the prices of a shopping cart that are saved on a list.

1. priceList = [10.99, 15.25, 11.00, 244.39] # List of prices.

2. totalPrice = 0 # variable to hold the total price.

3. **for** price **in** priceList: #
   Note that you can call your variable any name that you want.

4.   totalPrice += price # Adding current list item to price.

5. **print**(totalPrice) # Printing the total price.

Program output:

C:\Users\...\PycharmProjects\GettingStarted\venv\Scripts\Python.exe
C:/Users/.../PycharmProjects/GettingStarted/MyFirstProgram.py
281.63

Process finished with exit code 0

Nested loops

Nested loops, in essence, are created by running two loops inside each other to create the desired outcome. We normally do this when we have a set of instructions that need to be run in blocks more than once. For this first example, we are going to list a set of coordinates using nested loops.

1. **for** x **in** range(5): #
   The first loop will create the x coordinates.

2.   **for** y **in** range(5): #
   The second loop will create the y coordinates.

3.   **print**(f'({x}, {y})') #
   This will print the coordinates as you would expect.

Program output:

```
C:\Users\...\PycharmProjects\GettingStarted\venv\Scripts\Python.exe
C:/Users/.../PycharmProjects/GettingStarted/MyFirstProgram.py
(0, 0)
(0, 1)
(0, 2)
(0, 3)
(0, 4)
(1, 0)
(1, 1)
(1, 2)
(1, 3)
(1, 4)
(2, 0)
(2, 1)
(2, 2)
(2, 3)
(2, 4)
(3, 0)
(3, 1)
(3, 2)
(3, 3)
(3, 4)
(4, 0)
(4, 1)
(4, 2)
(4, 3)
(4, 4)
Process finished with exit code 0
```

Chapter 6

Functions

Another cornerstone of programming are the functions. Unlike the built-in ones that are ready to go once you've started, user-defined functions open up unlimited possibilities. Using functions helps programmers abstract their code and simplify modifications in the future. Think of it as a container which is labeled and will only run once you call it, making it perfect for event-driven programming. In this chapter, we are going to take a closer look at how to create, alter, and place functions to get the most out of your programs.

Definition statement and Function Calls

There is a distinct method to define a function. The syntax of that is in the code that follows. In this hypothetical example, we will be creating a function that will square a given number.

1. **def** greetUser(): #
   Definition statement starts with def which is reserved, followed by the function name.

2.   purpose = input('State your purpose: ')
     #First line of the code block.

3.   **print**(purpose) # Second line of the code block.

4.

5.

> #For good code writing practices, you should add two empty lines (breaks) after your function bloc.

6. **print**('You have reached the umbrella corporation website') #This is the first thing that will run in the program.

7. greetUser() #The function will only run after you call it like that (name of the function followed by parenthesis).

Program output:

```
C:\Users\...\PycharmProjects\GettingStarted\venv\Scripts\Python.exe
C:/Users/.../PycharmProjects/GettingStarted/MyFirstProgram.py
You have reached the umbrella corporation website
State your purpose: I'm looking for Alice...
I'm looking for Alice...

Process finished with exit code 0
```

As explained previously, programs will run in a sequence of lines, so line one will be followed by line two, and so on. For that same reason, a function needs to be defined before calling it. If you try and call a function ahead of time, your IDE will prompt you with an error.

Parameters

Now let's explore how to add parameters to our functions. In many cases, we need to take information from the user or elsewhere and use it inside of a function. This technique is used by all programmers, regardless of what kind of program they are creating. Follow the instructions below to see how it works.

1. **def** greetUser(userName): #This is the parameter that we pass when the function is called on lines 7 and 8.

2.   purpose = input('State your purpose: ')

3.   **print**(f'Hello {userName.title()}, are these your intentions: "{purpose}" ?')

   # Here we are using the parameter.

   # We are also using the title method, to avoid any user error.

4.

5.

6. **print**('You have reached the umbrella corporation website') #This is the first thing that will run in the program.

7. greetUser("rEbEcEa") # Once you have added a parameter you need to supply a value while calling the function.

8. greetUser("dr. Green") # Each time you call a function, the new parameter is passed.

Program output:

```
C:\Users\...\PycharmProjects\GettingStarted\venv\Scripts\Python.exe
C:/Users/.../PycharmProjects/GettingStarted/MyFirstProgram.py
You have reached the umbrella corporation website
State your purpose: I'm looking for Alice
Hello Rebecea, are these your intentions: "I'm looking for Alice"?
```

```
State your purpose: Create a virus!
Hello Dr. Green, are these your intentions: "Create a virus!"?


Process finished with exit code 0
```

Keyword Arguments

In most cases, you may be passing more than one parameter into your program. In cases like these you need to pass the value of these parameters with respect to how they were defined in the function. Let's see an example.

1. **def** greetUser(firstName, lastName):

2.   purpose = input('State your purpose: ')

3.   **print**(f'Hello {firstName.title()} {lastName.title()}, are these your intentions: "{purpose}" ?')

4.

5.

6. **print**('You have reached the umbrella corporation website')

7. greetUser("rebecca", "chambers") #In this function call we have the first name as the first parameter.

8. greetUser('chambers', 'rebecca') #In this function call we have the last name as the first parameter

Program output:

```
C:\Users\...\PycharmProjects\GettingStarted\venv\Scripts\Python.exe
C:/Users/.../PycharmProjects/GettingStarted/MyFirstProgram.py
```

In rare cases, a programmer will need to pass parameters out of order. Although this is not always recommended, there are cases where it is necessary. To do that, all you have to do is add the parameter name while calling the function. Let's take a look at the next example.

1. **def** greetUser(firstName, lastName):

2.   purpose = input('State your purpose: ')

3.   **print**(f'Hello {firstName.title()} {lastName.title()}, are these your intentions: "{purpose}" ?')

4.

5.

6. **print**('You have reached the umbrella corporation website')

7. greetUser("rebecca", "chambers") #In this function call, we have the first name as the first parameter.

8. greetUser('chambers', 'rebecca') #In this function call, we have the last name as the first parameter

9. greetUser(lastName = 'chambers', firstName='Rebecca') #We swapped the order and still were able to pass the parameters as desired.

82

Program output:

```
C:\Users\...\PycharmProjects\GettingStarted\venv\Scripts\Python.exe
C:/Users/.../PycharmProjects/GettingStarted/MyFirstProgram.py
You have reached the umbrella corporation website
State your purpose: Saving Alice
Hello Rebecca Chambers, are these your intentions: "Saving Alice" ?
State your purpose: Saving Alice
Hello Chambers Rebecca, are these your intentions: "Saving Alice" ?
State your purpose: Saving Alice
Hello Rebecca Chambers, are these your intentions: "Saving Alice" ?

Process finished with exit code 0
```

Return values

There are many cases where you will take a piece of information from the user, run a function and need to return that value to the user again. It is very simply done by writing 'return' in front of the variables you wish to return. In this next example, we are going to create a very simple function that will calculate the square of any number and return the value to the user.

1. **def** squareNum(numA): # Parameter

2.   **return** numA *numA #
   Add the return at the beginning or else, by default, it will return none.

3.

4. **print**(squareNum(3)) #Note that the function was called as an argument and it can also be saved into a variable if necessary.

Program output:

```
C:\Users\...\PycharmProjects\GettingStarted\venv\Scripts\Python.exe
C:/Users/.../PycharmProjects/GettingStarted/MyFirstProgram.py
9

Process finished with exit code 0
```

Chapter 7

Conditional Statements

One of the pillars of programming is the ability to let computers make decisions based on information. In this chapter, we will tackle the different ways that we can tell a computer to act in a certain way. One of the things that you need to know is the fact that programming is sequential. Think about it as time-travel; you cannot know what you have not experienced. It works the same way with programs. If you have not predefined a condition, the computer will either ignore you or will hit you with an annoying error. At this point, it is important to mention that computers can only follow precise instructions, as a computer will not be able to understand variables that are not predefined. This is different when it comes to neural networks and artificial intelligence, and luckily for you, Python is one of the best programming languages when it comes to these two disciplines. That said, this particular book does not cover either. You will have to embark on another adventure in an advanced course later on.

If Statements

Probably the most well-known condition is the 'if statement', which does exactly what it says. In this statement, you prepare a condition and, if it is met, then a certain action is taken. If it is not met, another action will be taken – in some cases, the other action is no action at all.

So, for example, let's say that you are creating a program that requires some sort of credentials from the user before they are granted access. This has traditionally been done with 'if statements.' However, nowadays, there are built-in functions that can do it for you. Regardless, we will take a trip down memory lane and get to do this ourselves later on. For now, let's explore a simpler task.

You decide to create a program that will give you advice on what to wear at any given day. Remember that your program is not a fortune teller, at least under the hood. You will need to map out all the alternatives for that particular undertaking. If the weather is hot, you would probably like to wear shorts and a t-shirt. If the weather is cold, you would need to wear pants and a jacket. In any other case, you'll opt for jeans and a shirt. Let's take a look at the first part of the program.

1. tooHot = True

2. **if** tooHot: # This is how make conditions of boolean variables.

3.   #Remember to press enter afterward to start the code block that will execute the True part of the statement

4.   **print**(f"It's hot out there, wear jeans and a t-shirt")

5.   # If you want to end the true part of the statement, press and hold shift, now press on tab once.

Program output

```
C:\Users\...\PycharmProjects\GettingStarted\venv\Scripts\Python.exe
C:/Users/.../PycharmProjects/GettingStarted/MyFirstProgram.py
It's hot out there, wear jeans and a t-shirt

Process finished with exit code 0
```

Now, let's add the rest of the function, where we will add the statement for the case of cold weather. What we'll do is add an 'else' after the first code block and then print out what should happen if the condition is not met.

1. tooHot = False #Change the variable to True or False, to see the results you expect.

2. **If** tooHot: #This is how to make conditions of Boolean variables.

3.   #Remember to press enter afterward to start the code block that will execute the True part of the statement.

4.   **print**(f"It's hot out there, wear jeans and a t-shirt")

5.   #
   If you want to end the true part of the statement, press and hold shift, now press on tab once.

6. **else**: # After typing 'else,' we press on enter.

7.   **print**(f"It's TOO cold!, wear some pants & a jacket ")
   #This will only run if our variable is set to false.

Program output:

```
C:\Users\...\PycharmProjects\GettingStarted\venv\Scripts\Python.exe
C:/Users/.../PycharmProjects/GettingStarted/MyFirstProgram.py
It's TOO cold!, wear some pants & a jacket

Process finished with exit code 0
```

Now that we have done that let's explore the third option. For this to work, we will need to add a second variable so that we can test the second condition. We will also use a new part of the statement called the 'else if.' The 'else if' will basically nest two 'if statements' together, creating a new degree to the condition. Think about it as the inception version of 'if statements.'

1. tooHot = False #Change the variable to True or False, to see the results you expect.

2. tooCold =False #Change the variable to True or False, to see the results you expect.

3. **If** tooHot: #This is how to make conditions of Boolean variables.

4.   #
Remember to press enter afterwards to start the code block that will execute the True part of the statement.

5.   **print**(f"It's hot out there, wear jeans and a t-shirt")

6.   # If you want to end the true part of the statement, press and hold shift, now press on tab once.

7. **elif** tooCold: # elif is short for else if.

8.   **print**(f"It's TOO cold!, wear some pants & a jacket ")
#This will only run if the too cold variable is set to true.

9. **else**: #This will only exectute if none of the above conditions are met.

10.   **print**(f"It's a lovely day, wear a pair of jeans and a shirt")

11. #Remember to press on shift tab once you are done with this code block to end the 'if statement.'

```
C:\Users\...\PycharmProjects\GettingStarted\venv\Scripts\Python.exe
C:/Users/.../PycharmProjects/GettingStarted/MyFirstProgram.py
It's a lovely day, wear a pair of jeans and a shirt

Process finished with exit code 0
```

Try and mess around with the variables some more to make sure that they work properly. It's good practice to map your 'if statements' before executing them. That can be done through a notepad or simply following the indentations that are used in Python. With time, 'if statements' will come as second nature.

Now let's try and use some math in our conditions. Let's imagine that you want to create a program that will calculate the down payment of a house. So, if the person's credit is good, they will pay 10%. Otherwise, they will pay 30%.

1. propertyPrice= 100000 # Price of the unit

2. customerCredit =True #Credit status True for good and False for bad.

3. **if** customerCredit:

4. downPayment = propertyPrice * 0.1

5. else:

6. downPayment = propertyPrice * 0.3 #Remember to press on Shift + Tab or it will not print when the credit is good.

7. **print**(f"The down payment is ${downPayment}") #This is a formatted string; we use the curly braces to include a variable

8. # Note that we used the same variable for both cases.

Program output:

```
C:\Users\...\PycharmProjects\GettingStarted\venv\Scripts\Python.exe
C:/Users/.../PycharmProjects/GettingStarted/MyFirstProgram.py
The down payment is $10000.0

Process finished with exit code 0
```

Did you notice that we used the same variable on both blocks? The program will run in either the true or false block. As a result, you can use the one variable and print out whatever the result is instead of adding a print function on each one of the blocks.

Here is a program that will determine if a number is positive, negative or zero. This involves a few nested Ifs and ends by printing a message to the console.

1. numA = int(input('Please enter a number: '))
   #Input a value and converting it to an integer

2. **if** numA < 0: # Condition number is smaller than zero

3.   numType = 'negative' # This will be displayed later.

4. # Do not forget to press on shift tab after pressing on enter.

5. **elif** numA == 0: #Double equal signs is to check if both sides are equal.

6.   numType = 'zero'

90

7. # Do not forget to press on shift tab after pressing on enter.

8. **elif** numA > 0: #Condition that the number is greater than zero.

9.   numType = 'positive'

10. # Do not forget to press on shift tab after pressing on enter.

11. else:

12.   **print**("That is not a number, I have no clue what you did!")

13. # Do not forget to press on shift tab after pressing on enter.

14. **print**(f"The number you entered {numA}, is {numType}.")

Program output:

```
C:\Users\...\PycharmProjects\GettingStarted\venv\Scripts\Python.exe
C:/Users/.../PycharmProjects/GettingStarted/MyFirstProgram.py
The number you entered 45, is positive.

Process finished with exit code 0
```

Logical Operators

Logical operators are used in situations where you have multiple conditions rather than just the one. Think about it as your picky friend who will not settle for anyone because the perfect match is not there. If that person is you, this section will be a breeze for you. Let's imagine that you want to create a program that establishes if you are entitled to get a prescription drug. Here, there are two conditions: The person needs to present identification as well as a prescription from the doctor. Look at the code below.

```python
1.  customerID = False

2.  customerPrescription = False

3.  if customerID and customerPrescription: #Note the 'and'
    between the two conditions. This is the operator.

4.      msg = f'You can buy this drug' #
    Message if meets both conditions.

5.  elif customerID: #Note that you are checking if the
    customer HAS an ID with him.

6.      msg = f'You need a prescription from the doctor'

7.      # Since the customer does not have both the ID and
    prescription and, the customer has the ID.

8.      # We can conclude that he does not have the prescription.

9.  elif customerPrescription:

10.     msg = f'You need to have your ID to buy this drug'

11.     # Customer does not have both together. Customer does not
    have his ID. Testing to see if he has a prescription

12. else:

13.     msg = f'Please provide both the prescription and this
    ID to buy the drug'

14. print(msg)
```

Program output:

C:\Users\...\PycharmProjects\GettingStarted\venv\Scripts\Python.exe
C:/Users/.../PycharmProjects/GettingStarted/MyFirstProgram.py
Please provide both the prescription and the ID to buy the drug

Process finished with exit code 0

Now try and change the variables to True and False. There are four variations of possibilities, so make sure that they are all working.

Next, let's take a look at other logical operators, the OR and NOT. Again, just as advertised, the OR looks to meet one of two conditions, not necessarily both. So let's say that you are creating a program for a shop where it will accept any form of payment between cash or credit card. However, the shop does not accept checks. Look at the code below and again do not forget to test the different variations when you are done.

1. payCash = True

2. payCC = False

3. payCheck = True

4. **if** (payCash **or** payCC) **and not** payCheck:
    #Condition with three operators.

5. #Note 1: By placing the OR conditions in parenthesis, we tell Python which arguments to process first.

6. #Note 2: By using not payCheck, we are testing the variable and looking for a False value.

93

7. #Note 3: You can use the NOT operator alongside OR as well as the AND.

8. msg = f'Acceptable payment method'

9. else:

10. msg = f'we apologize but, checks are not accepted'

11. **print**(msg)

Program output:

```
C:\Users\...\PycharmProjects\GettingStarted\venv\Scripts\Python.exe
C:/Users/.../PycharmProjects/GettingStarted/MyFirstProgram.py
we apologize but checks are not accepted

Process finished with exit code 0
```

Comparing Operators

In this section, we have a small matrix with the logical operators that can be used in Python.

Operator	Description	Example
and	If the two operands are true then the condition becomes true.	numA and numB == 10
or	If either of the two operands are true then the condition becomes true.	numA or numb < 10
not	If the operands are not true then the condition is true.	not numA == 10

Chapter 8

Local and Global Scopes

After learning about functions and understanding the importance of using them, we are going to take another look at variables. In this section, let us stream through the differences between variables declared inside a function and variables that are declared normally – i.e., local and global variables.

In principle, variables should be declared only when needed. Back in the day, programmers used to declare all of their variables at the very beginning of their algorithm. This led to an increase in the load time of any particular program. More importantly, this meant that the running program was wasting processing power and memory space on variables that may not be used at all. This started to change bit by bit after the diffusion of graphical user interfaces and event-driven programming.

Global variables

For this particular book, we will define a global variable as one that can be reached throughout the whole program. In other words, it is not part of a block of code that will only run under certain conditions. The art of establishing you're global variables does not entirely rely on the programs functionality. You should also be concerned with security risks as well as privacy concerns when it comes to data. Think. Yes, think carefully about the variables that you are declaring globally and keep in mind who will have access to that variable. We don't want a password saved as a global variable, where anyone with minor skills and will can access it. Here is an example of a global variable.

1. # This function uses global variables.

2. **def** carSale(): #This function will only run when it is called in line 8

3.   **print**(f'$ {price}') #Practically the price variable is declared before this print function.

4.

5.

6. # Global scope

7. price = 120000

8. carSale()

Program output:

```
C:\Users\...\PycharmProjects\GettingStarted\venv\Scripts\Python.exe
C:/Users/.../PycharmProjects/GettingStarted/MyFirstProgram.py
$120000

Process finished with exit code 0
```

Local variables

Local variables are the opposite. These are variables that will only work within a particular scope or code block. This means that it can only be accessed and manipulated within a certain block of code. These tend to be useful as they are automatically erased from the computer's memory as soon as the function is finished executing. Moreover, it is a safer place to keep sensitive and private information as the variables only surface on demand. Let's take a look at a local variable.

1. # This function uses global variables.

2. **def** carSale(): #This function will only run when it is called in line 7

3. price = 150000 #The price variable is declared locally, that means it cannot be accessed outside of the function.

4. **print**(f'Local variable price : $ {price}')

5.

6.

7. carSale()

8. **print**(f'$ {price}') # Here is an attempt to access the variable price globally - it will produce an error -.

Program output:

```
C:\Users\...\PycharmProjects\GettingStarted\venv\Scripts\Python.exe
C:/Users/.../PycharmProjects/GettingStarted/MyFirstProgram.py
Local variable price : $150000
Traceback (most recent call last):
  File "C:/Users/.../PycharmProjects/GettingStarted/MyFirstProgram.py",
line 8, in <module>
```

```
    print(f'$ {price}') # Here is an attempt to access the variable price
globally - it will produce an error.
NameError: name 'price' is not defined

Process finished with exit code 1
```

The error that the program has prompted is one stating that it cannot find a variable called 'price.' This should show you how important it is to determine which variables should only be used locally and which ones should be used globally.

Local versus global variables

Now that we have established the difference between the two variables, we will start exploring how they interact. In this first example, we will see what happens when we have a local and a global variable of the same name.

1. # Local scope

2. **def** carSale():

3.   price =150000 # Local variable

4.   **print**(f'This is the local variable price (${price})')
       #Printing local variable

5.

6.

7. # Global scope

8. price = 120000

9.   carSale()

10. **print**(f'This is the global variable price (\${price})')
     #Printing global variable

Program output:

```
C:\Users\...\PycharmProjects\GettingStarted\venv\Scripts\Python.exe
C:/Users/.../PycharmProjects/GettingStarted/MyFirstProgram.py
This is the local variable price ($150000)
This is the global variable price ($120000)

Process finished with exit code 0
```

As you see in the program above, the price variable was printed with two different values. If we trace the program line by line, you will see that the local variable takes precedence while it is running the function. That is why we see the first output to match the value of the local variable. Meanwhile, the global variable does not get replaced. It is available and accessible once you have broken away from the code block of the function.

Now let's see what happens if we define the price variable after attempting to print.

1.   **def** carSale():

2.   **print**(f'This is the local variable price (\${price})')
       #Attempting to printing local variable

3.   price = 150000 #Local variable #Program will not produce an error if this line is removed.

4.

5.

6. # Global scope

7. price = 120000

8. carSale()

9. **print**(f'This is the global variable price (${price})')
   #Printing global variable

Program output:

```
C:\Users\...\PycharmProjects\GettingStarted\venv\Scripts\Python.exe
C:/Users/.../PycharmProjects/GettingStarted/MyFirstProgram.py
Traceback (most recent call last):
  File "C:/Users/.../PycharmProjects/GettingStarted/MyFirstProgram.py",
line 8, in <module>
    carSale()
  File "C:/Users/.../PycharmProjects/GettingStarted/MyFirstProgram.py",
line 2, in carSale
    print(f'this is the local variable price (${price})')  # Attempting to
printing local variable
UnboundLocalError: local variable 'price' referenced before assignment

Process finished with exit code 1
```

In this case, even though we had both a global and a local variable defined, the Python terminal still prompted an error stating that the variable was defined after attempting to reach it. Not any later. Interestingly, if you remove line three altogether, it will not produce an error message. Think of the local variable as its own bubble, a pocket universe of its own with its own governing laws of physics. Let us put it in a better way: A function can be considered as a small program within a bigger program. Python will treat the function's block of code as such.

Global Statement

There are cases where you would like to alter or use a global variable inside a function block. So, if you want to use a global variable while using a local one, you must use a reserved keyword 'global'. The following example should make it clearer.

1. **def** carSale():

2.   **global** price #We are using the keyword to access the global variable.

3.   **print**(f'This is the global variable price (${price})')
   #Printing global variable

4.   price = 150000 #Local variable
   #Program will not produce an error if this line is removed.

5.   **print**(f'This is the local variable price (${price})')
   #Printing local variable

6.

7.

8. # Global scope

9. price = 120000

10. carSale()

Program output:

```
C:\Users\...\PycharmProjects\GettingStarted\venv\Scripts\Python.exe
C:/Users/.../PycharmProjects/GettingStarted/MyFirstProgram.py
This is the global variable price ($120000)
This is the local variable price ($150000)

Process finished with exit code 0
```

Chapter 9

Exception Handling

In this section, we will go through handling errors in any Python program. This is a pillar part of programming, especially when you are dealing with user errors. If you are oblivious that you have errors, then they will never be handled or solved. Let's start with a basic question: When do I know there is an error? To understand that, let us run a simple program where we take information from the user. We ask the user to input something like his date of birth.

1. # Start program

2. **def** getBirthYear():
    #This function is here to gather the birth year of the user.

3. birthYear = int(input('What is your birth year? '))
    #Saving user input as an integer inside a variable.

4. **print**(birthYear)

5.

6.

7. getBirthYear() # Calling the getBirthYear year function.

Program output:

```
C:\Users\...\PycharmProjects\GettingStarted\venv\Scripts\Python.exe
C:/Users/.../PycharmProjects/GettingStarted/MyFirstProgram.py
What is your birth year? 1982
1982


Process finished with exit code 0
```

This program seems to be completely suitable as long as the user enters a number. What if the user decides to use letters instead of numbers? Using the same exact program, take a look at the message that we would get in the terminal.

Program output:

```
C:\Users\...\PycharmProjects\GettingStarted\venv\Scripts\Python.exe
C:/Users/.../PycharmProjects/GettingStarted/MyFirstProgram.py
What is your birth year? Nineteen eighty two
Traceback (most recent call last):
  File "C:/Users/.../PycharmProjects/GettingStarted/MyFirstProgram.py",
line 7, in <module>
    getBirthYear() # Calling the getBirthYear year function.
  File "C:/Users/.../PycharmProjects/GettingStarted/MyFirstProgram.py",
line 3, in getBirthYear
    birthYear = int(input('What is your birth year? '))  # Saving user input
as an integer inside a variable.
ValueError: invalid literal for int() with base 10: 'Ninetenn eighty two'

Process finished with exit code 1
```

The output console is telling you that the information gathered from the user is a string and cannot convert it to a valid number. As a result of this user input, the whole program has crashed and would not continue to work. The last line of the console output states that, "The process finished with exit code 1." Any exit code that is not zero means that your program has crashed. In the upcoming section we will see how we can prevent this from happening.

Raising exceptions

We will try and fix our code by adding an exception. What we need to do is use a 'try and except' statement that will not let our program crash. Let's take a look at how this is done.

1. Start program

2. **def** getBirthYear():
   #This function is here to gather the birth year of the user.

3.   **try**: #This will start the exception statement to try the next block of code.

4.   birthYear = int(input('What is your birth year? '))
   #Saving user input as an integer inside a variable.

5.   **print**(birthYear)

6.   **except** ValueError: # In the case that we get an error because of a value, we want to execute this next line of code.

7.   **print**(f'You need to enter a number, words and spaces are not acceptable') # error message

8.

9.

10. getBirthYear() # Calling the getBirthYear year function.

Program output:

```
C:\Users\...\PycharmProjects\GettingStarted\venv\Scripts\Python.exe
C:/Users/.../PycharmProjects/GettingStarted/MyFirstProgram.py
What is your birth year? Nineteen Eight Two
You need to enter a number, words and spaces are not acceptable

Process finished with exit code 0
```

Last time we ran our code, the program crashed with a Value Error. In this case, we added an exception to first try the block of code, and if a value error shows up, to display the message below. If you look at the exit code in the last line of the console output, you will find that it is a zero. Not only did we inform the user what they need to do, but we have also managed to stop our program from crashing.

Now again, using the same program let us expand it a bit, by asking our user to input the annual income. After that, we will calculate the user's age and divide the income by age. In this first scenario, the user will input integers in both cases.

1. # Start program

2. **def** getAverageIncome():
    #This function is here to calculate the average income.

3.   **try**: #This will start the exception statement to try the next block of code.

4.   age = int(input('How old are you? ')) #Saving user input as an integer inside a variable.

5.   userIncome = int(input("What's your annual income? ")) #Saving user input as an integer inside a variable

6.   averageIncome =round(userIncome / age) #Rounding the output to get a natural number.

7.   **print**(f"You've made an average of \${averageIncome} per year") # Printing the outcome.

8.   **except** ValueError: #In the case that we get an error because of a value, we want to execute this next line of code.

9.   **print**(f'You need to enter a number, words and spaces are not acceptable')

10.

11.

12. getAverageIncome() #Calling the getAverageIncome function.

Program output:

```
C:\Users\...\PycharmProjects\GettingStarted\venv\Scripts\Python.exe
C:/Users/.../PycharmProjects/GettingStarted/MyFirstProgram.py
How old are you? 1982
What's your annual income? 60000
You've made an average of $1622 per year

Process finished with exit code 0
```

The program has run without any errors and was able to create the desired output. Now, let's test out adding a string into our new input in line 6. We should still get an exception just as we did before, stating that we need to enter a number.

Program output:

```
C:\Users\...\PycharmProjects\GettingStarted\venv\Scripts\Python.exe
C:/Users/.../PycharmProjects/GettingStarted/MyFirstProgram.py
How old are you? 1982
What's your annual income? $60,000
You need to enter a number, words and spaces are not acceptable


Process finished with exit code 0
```

Our code seems to be running well, without getting any undesired exit codes. What if the user enters an age of zero? Technically, it is a number, but you can't really divide anything by zero; it makes no sense. Let's see how our interpreter would handle a situation like this.

Program output:

```
C:\Users\...\PycharmProjects\GettingStarted\venv\Scripts\Python.exe
C:/Users/.../PycharmProjects/GettingStarted/MyFirstProgram.py
How old are you? 0
What's your annual income? 60000
Traceback (most recent call last):
  File "C:/Users/.../PycharmProjects/GettingStarted/MyFirstProgram.py",
line 12, in <module>
    getAverageIncome()  # Calling the getAverageIncome function.
```

```
File "C:/Users/.../PycharmProjects/GettingStarted/MyFirstProgram.py",
line 6, in getAverageIncome
    averageIncome =round( userIncome / age)  #Rounding the output to
get a natural number.
ZeroDivisionError: division by zero
Process finished with exit code 1
```

As you see we got a new kind of error, the zero division error. That means that we need to create another exception for that particular problem. In the following script, you will find another exception to our code.

1. # Start program

2. **def** getAverageIncome(): #This function is here to calculate the average income.

3.   **try**: #This will start the exception statement to try the next block of code.

4.   age = int(input('How old are you? ')) #Saving user input as an integer inside a variable.

5.   userIncome = int(input("What's your annual income? ")) #Saving user input as an integer inside a variable

6.   averageIncome = round(userIncome / age) #Rounding the output to get a natural number.

7.   **print**(f"You've made an average of ${averageIncome} per year") # Printing the outcome.

8.   **except** ValueError: #In the case that we get an error because of a value we want to execute this next line of code.

9. **print**(f'You need to enter a number, words and spaces are not acceptable')

10. **except** ZeroDivisionError:

11. **print**(f'You cannot be ZERO years old, please tell us how old are you? ')

12.

13.

14. getAverageIncome() # Calling the getAverageIncome function.

Program output:

```
C:\Users\...\PycharmProjects\GettingStarted\venv\Scripts\Python.exe
C:/Users/.../PycharmProjects/GettingStarted/MyFirstProgram.py
How old are you? 0
What's your annual income? 60000
You cannot be ZERO years old, please tell us how old are you?

Process finished with exit code 0
```

There is an urban legend about online banking that has been rumored for years amongst programmers and the IT industry. A man was attempting to transfer some funds to his wife's account using his internet banking service. They both had accounts in the same bank, and he tried something out of the box. Instead of typing the number 500, he typed -500. To his astonishment, his account was credit with $500 that belonged to his wife.

Unfortunately, to this day, we have not been able to trace any sources for this story. Regardless, this is an issue that can be resolved with one of two ways. Either raise an exception – the right way – or get an absolute value from the customer.

Traceback as a string

When an error occurs in Python, it generates information about how the error occurred, a process known as a traceback. The data generated includes bits of information that can become useful in understanding how the program crashed. The information provided includes the list below, and it is called the 'call stack':

- The error message

- The line number that caused the error

- The sequence of functions that caused the error

In this next example, we will intentionally raise an error through a couple of functions.

```
1.  def calculateFun():
2.      addActivity()
3.
4.
5.  def addActivity():
6.      raise Exception('This does not seem to be a number')
7.
8.
9.  calculateFun()
```

Program output:

```
C:\Users\...\PycharmProjects\GettingStarted\venv\Scripts\Python.exe
C:/Users/.../PycharmProjects/GettingStarted/MyFirstProgram.py
Traceback (most recent call last):
  File "C:/Users/.../PycharmProjects/GettingStarted/MyFirstProgram.py",
line 9, in <module>
    calculateFun()
  File "C:/Users/.../PycharmProjects/GettingStarted/MyFirstProgram.py",
line 2, in calculateFun
    addActivity()
  File "C:/Users/.../PycharmProjects/GettingStarted/MyFirstProgram.py",
line 6, in addActivity
    raise Exception('This does not seem to be a number')
Exception: This does not seem to be a number

Process finished with exit code 1
```

From the traceback, we can see that the error happened in line 9 at the 'calculateFun()' function, which calls in line 2 the 'addActivity()' function. In turn, it raised the exception in line 6. By using the call back you can identify the origin of the error when working in a program with nested functions.

You can obtain that information by importing the traceback module and then calling the *traceback.format_exc()*. Not only that, but if you don't want your program to crash, you can use an except statement and still be able to trace the error. Additionally, you can save the information in a log file and keep the program up and running. Let's take a look at how to do that.

1. **import** traceback # Importing the traceback module.

2.

3. **try**: # Try statement.

4.   **raise** Exception('This is an error message.')
   #The exception raised.

5. **except**: # except statement.

6.   errorFile = open('errorInfo.txt', 'w')
   #This will open a file with writing pillages.

7.   errorFile.write(traceback.format_exc())
   #This runs the traceback function and writes it on the file.

8.   errorFile.close() # This will close the file.

9.   **print**('The traceback info was written to errorInfo.txt.')
   #This will print the raised exception error.

Program output:

```
C:\Users\...\PycharmProjects\GettingStarted\venv\Scripts\Python.exe
C:/Users/.../PycharmProjects/GettingStarted/MyFirstProgram.py
The traceback info was written to errorInfo.txt.

Process finished with exit code 0
```

Assertions

An assertion is an error that a developer choses to produce as a form of a fact check. While building programs, the programmer assumes certain variables to have a certain value. When testing them, small things like a value of a variable may be changed after a few too many lines of code.

The syntax of an assertion is as follows:

i. The assert keyword

ii. A condition

iii. A string to display when the condition is False

For example, the following program will check and see if the garage door is closed.

1. GarageDoor = True #This indicates that the door is closed by having it as lost.

2. #The assert statement follows, giving you the knowledge that a value is not as intended.

3. **assert** GarageDoor == False, 'The Garage door must be closed at all times.' # The assert statement is set to False.

Program output:

```
C:\Users\...\PycharmProjects\GettingStarted\venv\Scripts\Python.exe
C:/Users/.../PycharmProjects/GettingStarted/MyFirstProgram.py
Traceback (most recent call last):
  File
"C:/Users/Ramy/PycharmProjects/GettingStarted/MyFirstProgram.py",
line 2, in <module>
    assert GarageDoor == False, 'The Garage door must be closed at all
times.'
AssertionError: The Garage door must be closed at all times.

Process finished with exit code 1
```

Chapter 10

Comments & Documentation

B elieve it or not, most of the time, people read the code rather than write it. Programmers write code for the users and developers - including yourself. You would be amazed at how many times programmers go through old code and find that they cannot understand their own programming. Now, imagine how other people feel when they are reading through your code.

In many cases, you will find yourself in a situation where you just need a block of code that works and need to adapt it to your own program. Unfortunately, a few too many libraries and programs do not have the suitable documentation to get that particular function up and running.

Commenting vs. documenting code

The difference between commenting and documenting is normally unclear to the novice. You should always think of your target audience, and that is the main distinction. In essence, commenting describes your code. It helps developers understand your code's design and purpose.

Documenting, on the other hand, should be tailored to your users with information about the functionality and use of the program itself. Developers will still need to read your documentation. No one really dives into code without any sort of description of what it does. However, this document is not primarily meant for them.

Commenting code basics

Comments are created using the hashtag "#" formally known as the pound sign. This should be very brief. All of the information below is based on the guide lines of PEP 8 mentioned in an earlier chapter. Please visit this link for complete explanations "https://pep8.org/#introduction".

Here's an example:

1. firstName='Nathan'

2. # This is a comment that precedes a print statement.

3. **print**(firstName)

Based on the PEP 8 guidelines, a comment should not exceed more than 72 characters. After that you should carry on with a comment in the line after. Don't worry, PyCharm has a ruler layered on your code that will tell you if you have exceeded the number of characters. Here is an example on how it is done.

1. firstName='Nathan'

2. #This is a comment that precedes a print statement.
   Here is a quote from monty Python "Black Knight:

3. # "Right, I'll do you for that!" King Arthur: 'You'll what?"
   Black Knight: "Come here!" King Arthur:

4. # "What are you gonna do, bleed on me?'"

5. **print**(firstName)1

One of the best things about commenting is how it is being used to plan and review your program. At the beginning of the code writing endeavor, you may consider planning out the code using comments. Then fill in the code between your main layouts as it helps you stay organized and helps when multiple developers are working on code.

1. # First step

2. # Second step

3. # Third step

Comments can be used to describe the intent of particular sections of code. This is done to facilitate the finding and understanding of blocks of code that connect externally or to different files. That's not to say that describing a function locally is wrong, on the contrary. It is actually encouraged.

1. #Attempt to login using user input. If successful redirect user to the cart. If unsuccessful prompt user to retry the

2. # Login process

In other cases, you should describe your algorithms if they are too complicated. Another good reason to place comments is to describe why you used a function, method, or library over another. Here is an example.

1. #Importing cmath module as complex numbers will be needed in this function.

Finishing a program in one go is very rare, especially the more features you add to your application. Tagging your code via comments helps remind you what it is that you need to work on and where.

1. #ToDo: add price as a global variable and set condition to see which the lowest price is. Pick the lowest as the cost.

Comments should be as brief as possible, or as brief as you are comfortable with. Here are a few tips when it comes to writing comments:

- Keep comments as close as possible to the code its describing.

- Don't use complex formatting such as tables.

- Don't include redundant information.

- Design the code to comment itself. Make it easy on the reader by using simple methods and descriptive variable names.

Fortunately, 'Type hinting' is a function built into Python from version 3.5 and it is quite simple to use. In most cases, it will hint to what is happening without the need to comment, and it is suggested automatically. Here is a sample of a few lines of code:

1. **def** greetingName(name: str) -> str:

2. **return** f"Hello {name}"

In the first line of code, the IDE has pointed out that the return value of this output will be a string.

Documentation formats

There are a variety of documentation formats that you can use. In the table, you will find quite a few that should help you chose. The recommended version for beginners is a format type called 'NumPi/ SciPy docstings'. In any case, you can chose whatever you are most comfortable with. Just remember to stick to one once you have started documenting a certain project.

Format Type	Description	Supported by Sphynx	Formal Specification	
i. Google Docstrings	Google's form of documentation	YES	NO	https://github.com/ google/styleguide/ blob/gh-pages/pyguide.md #38-comments-and-docstrings
ii. reStructured text	Official Python documentation standard (Feature rich).	YES	YES	http://docutils.sour ceforge.net/rst.htm l
iii. NumPi/ SciPy docstings	A combination of Google Docstrings & reStructured	YES	YES	https://numpydoc.r eadthedocs.io/en/la test/format.html
iv. EpyText	An adaptation of EpyDoc	NO	YES	http://epydoc.sourc eforge.net/epytext. html

As mentioned earlier, the main focus of the documentation is to be directed to the users. Surely, projects come in different ways, shapes, and sizes, but in principle, the main structure of documentation should be as follows:

119

```
project_root/
|
├── project/  # Project source code
├── docs/
├── README
├── HOW_TO_CONTRIBUTE
├── CODE_OF_CONDUCT
├── examples.py
```

Generally, projects can be categorized into three different types:

- Private projects

- Shared projects

- Public projects (Open source)

Documenting private projects

These are normally projects that are used privately, intended for personal use, and are not normally shared with other users or developers. You should add two parts to the normal documentation to this part. The first one is a Python script file called examles.py, and the second a brief summary in the readme file. Put in mind that this documentation is meant for the user - even if the only user is going to be yourself. Try and document anything that may be confusing.

Recommended parts to add	Description
i. Readme	This is a brief summary of the project's purpose, along with minimal requirements for use.
ii.examples.py	A Python script file that shows how to use the project by the use of simple examples.

https://realPython.com/documenting-Python-code/#documenting-your-Python-projects

Documenting shared projects

Shared projects are those where you collaborate with other developers or users. This can be colleagues at work, partners, or even a client. While documenting such projects, you need to be a bit more meticulous than a private project's documentation. You need to put in mind that other users and developers may need to understand, and in some cases alter, sections of the code that you wrote. Here are the sections that we recommend to add along with the normal documentation structure.

Recommended parts to add	Description
i. Readme	This is a brief summary about the project's purpose, along with any minimal requirements for use. Also, add any major changes since the previous version.
ii.examples.py	A Python script file that shows how to use the project by use of simple examples.
iii. How to contribute	This should explain how new contributors to the project can do so.

At the end of the day, just like coding, you will get better at documentation as you practice more and more. Don't worry if your documentation is good or bad. Having it is definitely better than having none.

Chapter 11

Classes and Objects

Classes are used in many programming languages, not just Python. So, if you have some background in any other language, you may have encountered classes before. For the uninitiated, using classes is defining other types of data. So far, we have discussed the basic types of data like Strings, Integers, floats, and Booleans, along with a bit more complex ones like lists and dictionaries. However, these types cannot always be used to model more complex concepts. For example, let's think about the concept of a shopping cart. It is not a Boolean, not a list, and not really any of the previously mentioned data types.

One of the strongest features about classes is the fact that you can create truly unique data types and use them as such. In other words, once a class is created, you can use it as if it were a data type with as many variables as you want. In our first example, we will create a new class called plotting points.

Creating a Class and an Object

A class can be created by placing a particular statement. According to PEP 8, classes should be named using the old Pascal naming convention. Pascal is an old programming language that named variables in pretty much the same way as the cammelcase but capitalizing both the first and next word. So, if I wanted to label a class as "user login", it would be called "UserLogin" instead of "userLogin". After creating a class, we will need to start creating objects. Think of a class as a blueprint or a mold that will be as many objects as you need. Here is an example below.

1. **class** PlottingPoints: # This is how we create a class.

2.   **def** move(self): #Defining a function within the class that will become a method to use.

3.   **print**(f'Move it, move it, move it! ')

4.

5.   **def** draw(self): #Defining a function within the class that will become a method to use.

6.   # The self

7.   **print**(f'Drawing the colors of the wind. ')

8. # Do not forget to use shift+tab to get out of the coding block.

Creating an object

We'll elaborate a bit more about what an object is. Imagine a class as a blueprint for a Swiss watch. The object would be the hundreds of watches that are created by those blueprints. These watches have different components in them, like the hour hand, minute hand, and so on. You can add attributes for a class by using a dot connotation and naming it, followed by an assignment (look at lines 12 and 13).

1. **class** PlottingPoints: # This is how we create a class.

2.   **def** move(self): #Defining a function within the class that will become a method to use.

3.   **print**(f'Move it, move it, move it! ')

4.

5.   **def** draw(self): #Defining a function within the class that will become a method to use.

6.   # The self

7.   **print**(f'Drawing the colors of the wind. ')

8.

9.

10. # Creating an object for our brand new class.

11. coordinate1 = PlottingPoints() #Creating an object inside of a variable called coordinate1.

12. coordinate1.x = 10 # Adding an attribute to our object.

13. coordinate1.y = 15 # Adding another attribute to our object.

14. **print**(f'({coordinate1.x}, {coordinate1.y})')

Program output:

```
C:\Users\...\PycharmProjects\GettingStarted\venv\Scripts\Python.exe
C:/Users/.../PycharmProjects/GettingStarted/MyFirstProgram.py
(10, 15)

Process finished with exit code 0
```

As you can see, the console has been able to print out two different attributes of the same variable. This is a game-changer! We no longer have to create a different variable every time we need to store something. It is all in one cozy complex variable.

In this next script, we will see two exclusive objects that are part of the same class.

1. # Creating a brand new class

2. **class** PlottingPoints: # This is how we create a class.

3.   **def** move(self): #Defining a function within the class that will become a method to use.

4.   **print**(f'Move it, move it, move it! ')

5.

6.   **def** draw(self): #Defining a function within the class that will become a method to use.

7.   # The self

8.   **print**(f'Drawing the colors of the wind. ')

9.   #Do not forget to use shift tab to get out of the coding block.

10.

11.

12. # Creating an object for our brand new class.

13. coordinate1 = PlottingPoints()

    #Creating an object inside ofa variable called coordinate1.

14. coordinate1.x = 10 # Adding an attribute to our object.

15. coordinate1.y = 15 # Adding another attribute to our object.

16. **print**(f'({coordinate1.x}, {coordinate1.y})')

17. # Creating a second object of the same class.

18. coordinate2 = PlottingPoints()

    #Same method of creatinganother object.

19. coordinate2.x = 55

    #This is a different value for a different object.

20. coordinate2.y = -6 # Adding another attribute to tour object.

21. **print**(f'({coordinate2.x}, {coordinate2.y})')

Program output:

```
C:\Users\...\PycharmProjects\GettingStarted\venv\Scripts\Python.exe
C:/Users/.../PycharmProjects/GettingStarted/MyFirstProgram.py
(10, 15)
(55, -6)

Process finished with exit code 0
```

Now that we have established that they work, why don't we take a look at why we created functions inside our object?

Object method

An object can have methods, which are basically functions that you can call on demand instead of having to redefine them every single time. For instance, there are objects that you know you will have to print over and over again. Instead of depending on a function that you must call every time you need to do that, you can simply define it in a class and add it as a method. Another great thing about methods is that they are embedded into the class and cannot be called if the object is not part of the class. This adds a layer of security that is great if you want to avoid well known vulnerabilities.

1. # Creating a brand new class

2. **class** PlottingPoints: # This is how we create a class.

3.   **def** move(self): #Defining a function within the class that will become a method to use.

4.   **print**(f'Move it, move it, move it! ')

5.

6.   **def** draw(self): #Defining a function within the class that will become a method to use.

7.   # The self

8.   **print**(f'Drawing the colors of the wind. ')

9.   #Do not forget to use shift tab to get out of the coding block.

10.

11.

12. # Creating an object for our brand new class.

13. coordinate1 = PlottingPoints()
    #Creating an object inside of a variable called coordinate1.

14. coordinate1.x = 10 # Adding an attribute to our object.

15. coordinate1.y = 15 # Adding another attribute to our object.

16. **print**(f'({coordinate1.x}, {coordinate1.y})')

17. # Creating a second object of the same class.

18. coordinate2 = PlottingPoints()
    #Same method of creating another object.

19. coordinate2.x = 55
    #This is a different value for a different object.

20. coordinate2.y = -6 # Adding another attribute to our object.

21. **print**(f'({coordinate2.x}, {coordinate2.y})')

22. # Using methods in our objects.

23. coordinate2.draw()
    #Using a method "draw" on the second object.

24. coordinate1.move()
    #Using a method "move" on the first object.

Program output:

```
C:\Users\...\PycharmProjects\GettingStarted\venv\Scripts\Python.exe
C:/Users/.../PycharmProjects/GettingStarted/MyFirstProgram.py
(10, 15)
```

As you can see, both methods do as intended and are able to execute our block of code just by using a dot connotation.

Another thing that is both useful and important is to initialize our object with the needed attributes. This will get our class ready. Knowing what it needs to expect as a result, it will be easier to enter information into the object.

1. # Creating a brand new class

2. **class** PlottingPoints: # This is how we create a class.

3.   #Adding the initializing method. This is a built in method that you can get by adding the two underscores.

4.   **def** __init__(self, XPosition, YPosition): #We are also going to add two parameters so that we can pass the

5.   # x Position & y Position into the correct place.

6.   self.XPosition = XPosition

7.   self.YPosition = YPosition

8.

9.   **def** move(self): #Defining a function within the class that will become a method to use.

129

10.   **print**(f'Move it, move it, move it! ')

11.

12.   **def** draw(self): #Defining a function within the class that will become a method to use.

13.   # The self

14.   **print**(f'Drawing the colors of the wind. ')

15.   #Do not forget to use shift tab to get out of the coding block.

16.

17.

18. # Creating an object for our brand new class.

19. coordinate1 = PlottingPoints(200, 200) #Placing parameters that will feed the method within the parenthesis.

20. **print**(f'({coordinate1.XPosition}, {coordinate1.YPosition})')

Program output:

```
C:\Users\...\PycharmProjects\GettingStarted\venv\Scripts\Python.exe
C:/Users/.../PycharmProjects/GettingStarted/MyFirstProgram.py
(200, 200)

Process finished with exit code 0
```

As you can see in line 19, we were able to create a new object as well as insert the values of the x and y positions within one line. This makes it easier to read. Also, it only creates the variables when needed on demand. Let's take another example before we move on. In this next situation, we want to create a new class that will store a person's name and will be able to greet that person via a method.

1. # Creating a class

2. **class** UserName:

3.   **def** __init__(self, PersonName):
    #Initializing variables within the class.

4.   self.PersonName = PersonName
    #Taking parameters and placing them in the object's variable.

5.

6.   **def** Greet(self): # Defining the Greet method.

7.   **print**(f'Welcome back {self.PersonName}!')
    #Printing the information required.

8.

9.

10. user1 = UserName('Jennifer')
    #Creating a new object and adding the PersonName parameter.

11. user1.Greet() # Calling the greet method for the first object.

12. user2 = UserName('Samantha') # Adding a second object.

13. user2.Greet() #Calling the greet method for the second object.

Program output:

```
C:\Users\...\PycharmProjects\GettingStarted\venv\Scripts\Python.exe
C:/Users/.../PycharmProjects/GettingStarted/MyFirstProgram.py
Welcome back Jennifer!
Welcome back Samantha!

Process finished with exit code 0
```

Chapter 12

Inheritance

This is another mechanism that is found in most programming languages that support classes allowing you to reuse the code. One of the big ideas in computer science generally is the notion of abstraction. Repeating code is just redundant and hard to maintain in the long run. Envision that we want to create two classes, one for pickup trucks and the other for SUVs. Generally, they are both cars and will have similar attributes. Instead of repeating the attributes in both classes we can make them inherit certain properties that both of them have in common.

Parent class

As discussed before, the parent class is the class that has attributes corresponding to any child class. In the example below, the parent class is the Cars class. That class has one attribute in common with all cars, and that is the CarDrive. As a result of the association created, both the SUVs and PickUp classes are able to call CarDrive as a method, even though they are not defined in their respective classes.

1. #Creating a parent class (this is exactly as a normal class no difference in syntax.

2. **class** Cars:

```
3.    def CarDrive(self):

4.        print(f'Vroom vroom!')

5.

6.

7.  # Creating a child class for SUVs

8.  class SUVs(Cars):  # By adding the class "Cars" into the SUVs
    class we are telling Python that we want to inherit the

9.      # Methods in the parent class.

10.   def __init__(self, Seats):

11.       self.Seats = Seats

12.

13.   def PrintSeats(self):

14.       print(f'This SUV can accommodate {self.Seats} people')

15.

16.

17. # Creating a child class for Pickups

18. class PickUp(Cars):

19.   def __init__(self, Size):

20.       self.Size = Size

21.

22.   def PrintSize(self):

23.       print(f'This Pickup has a trunk size of {self.Size}
    square feet.')
```

24.

25.

26. # Output of an object in the Pickup class.

27. car1 = PickUp(3)

    #Creating object and adding trunk size as a parameter.

28. car1.PrintSize()

    #Using the PrintSize method unique to the PickUp class.

29. car1.CarDrive()

    #Using the CarDrive method inherited from the Cars class.

30. # Output of an object in the SUV class.

31. car2 = SUVs(5) #Adding number of passengers as a parameter.

32. car2.PrintSeats()

    #Using the PrintSeats method unique to the SUVs class.

33. car2.CarDrive()

    #Using the CarDrive method inherited from the Cars class.

Program output:

```
C:\Users\...\PycharmProjects\GettingStarted\venv\Scripts\Python.exe
C:/Users/.../PycharmProjects/GettingStarted/MyFirstProgram.py
This Pickup has a trunk size of 3 square feet.
Vroom vroom!
This SUV can accommodate 5 people
Vroom vroom!


Process finished with exit code 0
```

Child class

A child class has the ability to inherit attributes from its parent class by adding the name of the parent class between the parentheses while declaring it. Additionally, the child class has the ability to have its unique attributes. One thing that you need to keep in mind is that Python will only allow a child class if the child class has a unique attribute. If you simply add the name of the parent class between the parentheses without any unique attributes, it will produce an error.

1. #Creating a parent class (This is exactly like a normal class; no difference in syntax).

2. **class** Cars:

3.   **def** CarDrive(self):

4.   **print**(f'Vroom vroom!')

5.

6.

7. # Creating a class for SUVs

8. **class** SUVs(Cars): # By adding the class "Cars" into the SUVs class we are telling Python that we want to inherit the

9. # No unique attributes will result in an error.

Program output:

```
C:\Users\...\PycharmProjects\GettingStarted\venv\Scripts\Python.exe
C:/Users/.../PycharmProjects/GettingStarted/MyFirstProgram.py
```

```
File "C:/Users/.../PycharmProjects/GettingStarted/MyFirstProgram.py",
line 10


                            ^

SyntaxError: unexpected EOF while parsing

Process finished with exit code 1
```

Sometimes, as programmers, we like to build the general layout of the program before filling in out functions, classes and whatnot. If there is a case where you need to do that, just use the pass statement in the child classes' block.

1. #Creating a parent class (this is exactly as a normal class no difference in syntax.

2. **class** Cars:

3.   **def** CarDrive(self):

4.   **print**(f'Vroom vroom!')

5.

6.

7. # Creating a class for SUVs

8. **class** SUVs(Cars): # by adding the class "Cars" into the SUVs class we are telling Python that we want to inherit the

9.   **pass** #The pass statement will ask the interpreter to neglect this line and continue.

```
C:\Users\...\PycharmProjects\GettingStarted\venv\Scripts\Python.exe
C:/Users/.../PycharmProjects/GettingStarted/MyFirstProgram.py
Process finished with exit code 0
```

Chapter 13

Modules

Modules are basically files with some Python code in them, and we use the module to organize the code into multiple files. This is a way to keep your code clean and well-classified. Just like when we walk into a pharmacy and find that they have all of their medicine placed in different drawers; we do the same in Python. No one wants to have one mega file 'app.py' with all of our functions and classes. What we do instead is simply break down pertinent parts into individual files. Think how much more productive would that be while working with a team. Also, how much easier it is to maintain the program as a whole; if you need to upgrade your payment features, you would just need to pull out that particular module (file) and update it. Moreover, given that Python is an open-source language, you can reuse and adapt modules with a simple import statement.

Creating a Module

As mentioned before, a module is simply a file. So, to begin creating a module, we simply need to create a file. To do that, we will maximize the project tool window, which is the left pane on PyCharm's interface. Now we will create a new file by right clicking on our project folder and selecting 'New', then clicking on 'File'. At this point we need to give our file a name followed by the dot py extension (example:

'convert.py'). Remember the general naming rules still apply; do not add spaces, special characters or reserved names. In our example, we are going to create a module that will have the ability to convert values from the empirical to the metric system.

convert.py

1. **def** mi2KM(miles):

2.   **return** round(miles * 1.609344) #Rounding up the kilometers calculated and returning the value.

3.

4. **def** km2MI(KM):

5.   **return** round(KM/1.609344)

#Rounding up the miles calculated and returning the value.

That is basically it. You just created a module, and you do not need to worry about anything in this file anymore. Just remember to only add functions for conversions in this file.

Using a module

In earlier chapters, we imported other built-in modules like 'math'. To be able to make your new module, just follow the same steps. Only this time, type 'import convert' instead of 'import math.' Note that we left out the file extension '.py' while importing the module.

MyFirstProgram.py

1. **import** convert # Importing the convert module.

2.

3. **print**(convert.km2MI(200))

   #Printing the result of the conversion.

4. **print**(convert.mi2KM(40))

   #Printing the other result of the conversion.

Program output:

```
C:\Users\...\PycharmProjects\GettingStarted\venv\Scripts\Python.exe
C:/Users/.../PycharmProjects/GettingStarted/MyFirstProgram.py
124
64

Process finished with exit code 0
```

Renaming a Module

Renaming a module is fairly simple and will only take one line of code. We use this kind of practice when we know that a certain module name will confuse the developers in a program. Let's say that you are creating a program that uses the label 'math' frequently. It could be a learning platform for kids where they practice math equations, for example. Anyway, you decide that you would like to rename the math module that you are going to import. That can be done by simply adding the word 'as' followed by the new name that you want to use.

1. **import** math as moo

   #Importing the math module and renaming it to moo.

2. c = 2 * moo.pi * 10 #Calculating the circumference of a circle.

3. **print**(c)   # Printing the result.

Program output:

```
C:\Users\...\PycharmProjects\GettingStarted\venv\Scripts\Python.exe
C:/Users/.../PycharmProjects/GettingStarted/MyFirstProgram.py
62.83185307179586

Process finished with exit code 0
```

Built-in modules

There is a plethora of modules, and it is constantly being updated and built into Python. Here is a cheat sheet that is available with documentation at this link "https://docs.Python.org/3/py-modindex.html".

As you progress in your programming abilities and build complex programs, these modules will make your life easier. There is absolutely no need to re-invent the wheel if the community has already given you plenty to work with.

One thing that you need to keep in mind is the structure of the program as a whole. Any non-trivial program will probably have three types of modules.

- The top-level file: This is the main file that is used to run all of your script and to launch the main application.

- User-defined modules: These are modules that have been created by the developer for specific use in the application.

- Standard library modules: These are modules that are built into Python and are not part of the executable itself (your program), but pertinent to the standard Python library.

The way complex programs should be built would consist of the top level file, which then calls the user-defined module. The standard Python modules should be called within the user defined ones. The figure below does not constitute the way you must design your program structure, but is simply an example of how sophisticated programs operate.

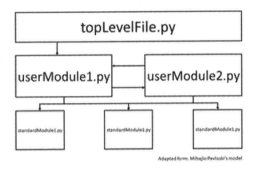

Adapted form: Mihajlo Pavlaski's model

Import from module

There are cases where you do not need to import complete modules, just specific functions in the module. Doing that is simple. We'll just use a slightly different syntax. This imports the function itself as if it were defined in the same file. There is no need for a dot notation in this case.

1. **from** convert **import** mi2KM

   #Importing a specific function from another module.

Printing the result of our function.

2. **print**(mi2KM(200))

   #Notice that the function is called as if it were

   defined in the same file.

Program output:

```
C:\Users\...\PycharmProjects\GettingStarted\venv\Scripts\Python.exe
C:/Users/.../PycharmProjects/GettingStarted/MyFirstProgram.py
322

Process finished with exit code 0
```

Chapter 14

Web Scraping

Web scraping is a term that can be used to mean that a program is online and starts performing actions. It could be as simple as opening a browser or as complex as the Google scrapping algorithm that gives us the answers to everything. There are a few modules that we can import and make our life easier when performing web-related actions.

- Requests: Downloads files and pages from the web.

- Webbrowser: Opens the browser to a specific URL.

- Beautiful Soup: It is able to parse (interpret) HTML.

Webbrowser Package

The first module that we will explore is the simplest. It just opens a URL for you. That's it. A lot of applications run this sort of command once you install a program or uninstall one. In some cases, you will need them if you want to refer your user to a web link. Here is a sample of how it's done, and it will result in opening the default browser to the URL address.

1. **import** webbrowser # Importing the webbrowser module.

2.

3. webbrowser.open('http://www.example.com') #Using the open method to launch the browser and navigate to the URL.

Now, let's get a bit more creative. In this next case, we will create a program that will take the user's address and add it to a Google Maps link. This way, the browser will automatically open to the person's Google Maps address. The only reason we can do this is because Google sets up its search query in the URL itself. If you open a browser and type in 'https://maps.google.com/place/Barcelona' or any other place you want, Google will do it for you.

To achieve that, we will first need to install a package called 'pyperclip 1.7.0'. In the run tool menu, click on the terminal tab at the very bottom. Now type this command: 'pip install pyperclip'

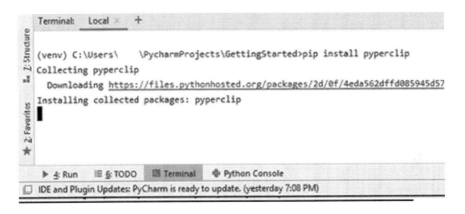

Wait for the 'download successful' message to show and click on the run tab that's on the left. Now let's take a look at the necessary code to achieve this.

1. **import** webbrowser, sys, pyperclip

2.

3. address=input('Please type in your address: ')
   # Get address using an input statement.

4. **if** len(address) < 1:
   #Checking to see if any character were written.

5.   address = pyperclip.paste() # Get address from clipboard.

6.

7. webbrowser.open('https://www.google.com/maps/place/' +
   address) # Opening browser with the address.

The program works in a very subtle way. After importing the required modules, it starts by prompting the user for an address. We could simply pass it to the webbrowser.open() method, and it will do that for you if you actually type an address. But where is the fun in that? So, instead, we have a simple if-statement that checks to see if the length of the characters is less than one. If it is, then we know that the user didn't type the address, and we take the address in the clipboard.

For this next exercise, we will need to install yet another module the 'requests 2.22.0'. To do that we will open the terminal again and type the following command 'pip install requests'. Once it has notified you that it's installed successfully, we're in business.

1. **import** requests

2.

3. res = requests.get('https://filingSystem.com/myTextFile.txt')
   # Downloading the text file

4. **print**(res.text[:250])
   #Printing the information inside of the text file.

Program output:

```
C:\Users\...\PycharmProjects\GettingStarted\venv\Scripts\Python.exe
C:/Users/.../PycharmProjects/GettingStarted/MyFirstProgram.py
This is a text file available online to test out the requests module.

Process finished with exit code 0
```

Beautiful Soup

Before we can take the web apart we will need to know some basic HTML. HTML stands for markup query language which is a language used to design websites. Here are a few links that can help you learn HTML.

    i. https://developer.mozilla.org/en-US/learn/html/

    ii. https://w3schools.com

    iii. https://khanacademy.org

Here are a few basics that you can use for now. This language has gained popularity throughout the nineties and started gaining real momentum by the turn of the millennium. Unlike Python, this markup language mostly structures and places aesthetic elements of the webpage. The greatest power of HTML is that it allows most other languages to manipulate those elements. Ordinarily, you will find that most websites have a mix of HTML, Cascade Style Sheets (CSS), JavaScript and another application language like PHP, Ruby, Visual Basic and so on.

Use your browser to see the code behind any website. In the example below, we are looking at Google's search engine. Do not let that scare you; we do not need to learn the language, just its basics. However, it would be beneficial if you learn it eventually.

```
<!doctype html>
<html itemscope itemtype="http://schema.org/WebPage" lang="en-EG">
▶<head>..</head>
▼<body jsmodel=" " class="hp vasq big" id="gsr">
  ▶<style>..</style>
  ▶<style data-jiis="cc" id="gstyle">..</style>
  ▶<style>..</style>
  ▼<div class="ctr-p" id="viewport">
    <div id="doc-info"></div>
    ▶<div id="cst">..</div>
    ▶<style>..</style>
    ▶<div id="gb" class="gb_T"></div>
    ▶<div class="jhp big" id="searchform">..</div>
    <div class="sfbg"></div>
    <div id="gac_scont"></div>
    ▶<dialog class="spch-dlg" id="spch-dlg">..</dialog>
    <div jscontroller="fEVM1C" style="display:none" data-v="0" jsdata="CAmuf;;Buduse" jsaction="rcuQ8h:np72mf"></div>
    ▼<div class="content" id="main">
      ▼<span class="ctr-p" id="body">
        ▼<center>
          ▶<div id="lga">..</div> == $0
          <div style="height:118px"></div>
          ▶<div id="prm-pt" style="margin-top:12px">..</div>
```

An HTML file always comes with a few core tags. The first one is an <HTML> tag, followed by a <head> tag and a <body> tag. A normal webpage structure should look something like this:

<html>
　　　<head>
　　　　　　<title> My Webpage</title>
　　　</head>
　　　<body>
　　　　　　<h1> Magnificent</h1>
　　　　　　<p> A completely <em>useless</em> website with no purpose what so ever.
　　　　　　</p>
　　　</body>
</html>

You can see the code of an HTML page by right clicking on any web page and selecting the 'view source code' item. There are other tools that you can use, like the browser developer tools. We may need to use this in a bit. However, for now, we'll move on. One thing that you should know at this point is that all of the markup languages are rendered at the browser. Meanwhile other programs like Python are rendered on the server. That means that the common users do not have access to the source code of your Python application.

Now we'll start using Beautiful Soup by importing it through the terminal button in the Run tool windows at the bottom of the page. Next, we'll need to type the command 'pip install bs4'.

1. import bs4, requests # Importing beautiful soup and requests.

2.

3. res = requests.get('http://dw.com') # Getting information from the DW website.

4. res.raise_for_status()

5. # Passing information into a variable

6. webText = bs4.BeautifulSoup(res.text, features="html.parser") #If you do not add the second parameter it will produce a warning.

Program output:

```
C:\Users\...\PycharmProjects\GettingStarted\venv\Scripts\Python.exe
C:/Users/.../PycharmProjects/GettingStarted/MyFirstProgram.py
Process finished with exit code 0
```

Now that we have selected our page, we have a few options to choose from. The table below represents the functions and methods that you can use with Beautiful Soup.

Select method	Description
soup.select('div')	Will select all of the division tags in the page.
soup.select('#main')	Will select the element with an id of 'main'.
soup.select('.layoutx')	Will select all elements that use the CSS class of '.layoutx'
soup.select('div p')	Will select all the paragraph elements within a division.
soup.select('div > p')	Will select all of the paragraph elements that are directly within a div.
soup.select('input[price]')	Will select all of the input elements that have a value of 'price'.
soup.select('input[type="button"]')	Will select input element with a type of button.

In this next example, we will use the select method to find a canvas element within a local html file.

1. import bs4

2.

3. file = open('index.html')
   #Opening an html file on the root directory

4. fileRead = bs4.BeautifulSoup(file.read(),

   features="html.parser") # Parsing the information in the file.

5. element = fileRead.select('p canvas')

   #Searching for a canvas element within a paragraph.

6. print(element)

Program output:

```
[<canvas id="mycanvas"></canvas>]

Process finished with exit code 0
```

In this program, we imported the Beautiful Soup module to open an existing html file in the computer. We then copied the object into a variable so we can access it. Note that if you do not add the features parameter, you will be prompted with an error. Finally, we make a specific selection about what it is that we want to find.

Chapter 15

Using CSV and Excel Spreadsheets

One of the tricks that you should definitely learn early on is how to manipulate and alter CSV files using any programming language. Eventually, most programmers get to learn how to do it the hard way, since it is such an important tool in the professional environment. Being able to manipulate spreadsheets is a huge plus that you should definitely master.

CSV stands for comma-separated values. This is a plain text file that separates its values with commas. We will need to install a special module so that we can use and access the information in a CSV file. Each line in the file represents a row, while each cell is separated by a comma. Here is a sample below. You can copy and paste it into notepad and then save it as 'ShopList.csv'. Now, copy the file inside the folder of your project.

12/14/2019,Wireless Adapters,21

12/15/2019,Keyboards,66

12/16/2019,RAM,15

12/17/2019,Printers,7

12/18/2019,Access Points,9

12/19/2019,Monitors,6

CSV files are not excel spreadsheets. There are many things that this file type cannot do. The list below has a few features that do not exist in CSV files:

- May not have images or charts embedded.
- May not specify cells' width and height.
- May not merge cells.
- Do not have multiple worksheets.
- Do not have different type values (It's always a string).
- Do not have settings for font size or color.

1. **import** csv # Importing the CSV module.

2.

3. file1 = open('Book1.csv')
   #Opening the CSV file and loading it into a variable.

4. file1Reader = csv.reader(file1)
   #Reading the file and saving it into a variable.

5. exampleData = list(file1Reader)
   #Placing row content into a list variable.

6. **print**(exampleData)
   #Printing the whole list inside the CSV file.

Program output:

```
C:\Users\...\PycharmProjects\GettingStarted\venv\Scripts\Python.exe
C:/Users/.../PycharmProjects/GettingStarted/MyFirstProgram.py
```

In this next example, we will extract the information from the CSV file and print it out, each row on a line of its own. The best way to achieve this is using a 'for loop' as it deals with strings quite comfortably.

1. **import** csv # Importing the CSV module.

2.

3. file1 = open('Book1.csv')
   #Opening the csv file and loading it into a variable.

4. file1Reader = csv.reader(file1)
   #Reading the file and saving it into a variable.

5. **for** row **in** file1Reader:
   #A 'for loop' to output all of the data in the CSV file.

6. **print**(f'Row # {str(file1Reader.line_num)} {str(row)}')
   #Printing the row number **and** the data within every row.

Program output:

154

In some cases, you will find that you need to write data into a CSV. Data is accessible as lists in most programs, and we want to keep a CSV file for other purposes like backing them up or sending a copy to a client. This is what we need to do.

1. **import** csv # Importing the csv module

2.

3. outputCSV = open('Backup.csv', 'w', newline='')
   #Opening the output file, with writing privilages.

4. writerCSV = csv.writer(outputCSV)
   #Identifying the variable where the module should write.

5. writerCSV.writerow(['Salt', 'Paprika', 'Oregano', 'Pepper'])
   #Writing the first line of values.

6. writerCSV.writerow(['Orange', 'Apple', 'Strawberry', 'Pear'])
   #Writing the next row of values.

7. outputCSV.close() # Closing the CSV file.

   Backup.csv file output:

   Salt,Paprika,Oregano,Pepper

   Orange,Apple,Strawberry,Pear

155

The script above imports the CSV module, then it opens the file with writing privileges by passing the 'w' and adds the new line argument. The reason why we add the new line argument is that if it is not added on its own. When running windows, you will find that your data has a double break. So one row of data, followed by an empty row, then followed by another row of data and so on. Doing that will create the object where you want, which you can use to write your data. The 'writerow' method will take a list argument and place each one in its own cell, as well as in the new line.

Sometimes, as programmers or IT personnel, we are given mundane tasks that are simply time consuming and beneath our skill level. For example, requesting to remove the headers of hundreds of CSV files. This is the kind of task that makes people want to run out of work and claim that they were never there. Luckily for us, we can automate that process using a few lines of code.

In this next example, we are going to assume that there are is undefined number of CSV files. The boss has asked you to remove the headers from all of them. We can do that by using a script like the one below.

1. **import** csv, os

2.

3. #This will create a file directory where the new copies will be saved.

4. os.makedirs('RemovingFirstRow', exist_ok=True)

5.

6. #This will create a loop that will check every file in the current directory.

7. **for** csvFile **in** os.listdir('.'):

8.   **if not** csvFile.endswith('.csv'):

9.   **continue** # Skip non-csv files

10.   **print**(f'Removing first row from {csvFile}...') #Printing the message for the user.

11.

12.   #Reading the CSV file.

13.   csvRows = [] # Creating a list variable.

14.   csvFileInstance = open(csvFile) # Opening the CSV file.

15.   csvReader = csv.reader(csvFileInstance) # Creating a reader object to use in the loop.

16.   **for** row **in** csvReader: #A loop to go through every line in the CSV

17.   **if** csvReader.line_num == 1: #The reader will do nothing if it is the first line of code.

18.   **continue** # Skip first row

19.   csvRows.append(row) #The reader will append any line that is not the first line.

20.   csvFileInstance.close() # Closing the file.

21.

22.   # Writing the replacement CSV files.

23. csvFileInstance = open(os.path.join('headerRemoved', csvFile), 'w', newline='') # Setting the write file name and directory with writing privileges and adding the newline argument to avoid double spaces.

24. csvWriter = csv.writer(csvFileInstance) #Writing in the object.

25. **for** row **in** csvRows:

26. csvWriter.writerow(row) #Writing the changes into the file.

27. csvFileInstance.close()

Program output:

```
C:\Users\...\PycharmProjects\GettingStarted\venv\Scripts\Python.exe
C:/Users/.../PycharmProjects/GettingStarted/MyFirstProgram.py
Removing first row from Grade 1 Class lists 2019-2020.csv...
Removing first row from Grade 2 Class lists 2019-2020.csv...
Removing first row from Grade 3 Class lists 2019-2020.csv...
Removing first row from Grade 4 Class lists 2019-2020.csv...
Removing first row from Grade 5 Class lists 2019-2020.csv...
Removing first row from Grade 6 Class lists 2019-2020.csv...
Removing first row from Grade 7 Class lists 2019-2020.csv...
Removing first row from Grade 8 Class lists 2019-2020.csv...
Removing first row from Grade 9 Class lists 2019-2020.csv...
Removing first row from Grade 10 Class lists 2019-2020.csv...
Removing first row from Grade 11 Class lists 2019-2020.csv...

Process finished with exit code 0
```

In this program, we start by importing both the 'csv' and 'os' modules. The 'os' module is used so you are able to make operating system actions like searching for folders, creating folders and so on. It is considered good practice to make copies of files that you are manipulating instead of modifying the ones that you have.

For that reason alone, the first thing we will do is create a new directory using the 'os' module. In line 3, you will find the os.makedirs() method – short for make directories - with two parameters in it. The first parameter is the name of the directory (folder), and the other parameter is to check if a directory exists. This is to avoid getting an error message by the program. We are simply telling the interpreter that if the file already exists, then do nothing.

In line 6, we have a 'for loop' to determine which of our files are CSV and which are not. We use the method of os.listdir(), and adding a period will get you only partway through. That is why we add an if statement to check if it is a CSV file. If it isn't, the computer will simply end without doing anything. Following that, a friendly message is displayed to tell the user that the files are being processed, identifying which files precisely on every cycle in the loop.

The next block of code begins on line 13, where we start reading the files that are on the root directory and are in fact CSV files. In line 14, we create a variable to store all of our information. We continue by opening the CSV file that is being inspected respective to their turn in the loop. Next, we read the data and place it in a variable using the csv.read() method. Now that we have the file ready for us, we'll create another loop that will read all of the rows inside the CSV file and append those rows.

159

The final block of code that starts in line 23 involves writing the gathered information into the new file. Just like reading the file, we will need to open our CSV file with writing privileges and finally writing all of the rows into the new file.

Installing the Openpyxl module

As discussed before, there are a bunch of third-party modules, also referred to as packages. In this section, we will dig a little bit deeper and use one of the most popular Python packages. CSVs are simple files that are easy to access, open, and use. However, using excel will always be superior due to all the functionality and aesthetics it provides.

To install the Openpyxl module, we need to download it from this link 'https://pypi.org/'. First we will need to search for Openpyxl in the search bar. In this book, we are using Openpyxl version 2.6.3. It is recommended that you use the same version to be able to follow the instructions. Click on the link that says Openpyxl 2.6.3 and look at the top left corner of the webpage. There will be the name of the package along with an install command below. Copy it.

Next, we need to type or paste that command into a terminal window. You will be able to find that inside of pyCharm as a tab in the 'Run tool Window' at the very bottom.

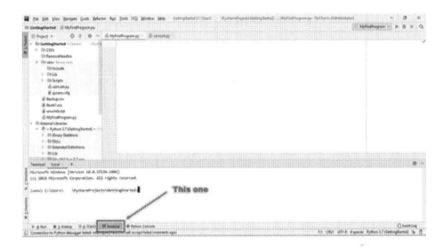

Once you have the terminal open, what we will need to do is paste the command that we saw on the webpage. Be patient because this may take some time depending on your internet speed.

Once it is finished, it will prompt the terminal command again. This means that you can now use this module, just like the built-in modules of Python.

Accessing and Altering Excel Documents

In this chapter, we explore how to deal with excel spreadsheets via Python. In this first section, we will learn how to load excel files and read specific sheets and cells. Find below the original file's content:

Rank	Movie name	Worldwide Gross (USD)
1	Titanic (1997)	1,845,034,188
2	The Lord of the Rings: The Return of the King (2003)	1,129,219,252
3	Pirates of the Caribbean: Dead Man's Chest (2006)	1,060,332,628
4	Harry Potter and the Philospher's Stone (2001)	976,475,550
5	Pirates of the Caribbean: At World's End (2007)	954,782,262
6	Star Wars Episode I: The Phantom Menace (1999)	924,300,000
7	The Lord of the Rings: The Two Towers (2002)	921,600,000
8	Shrek 2 (2004)	920,665,658
9	Jurassic Park (1993)	914,700,000
10	Harry Potter and the Goblet of Fire (2005)	892,194,397
11	Spider-Man 3 (2007)	890,065,018
12	Harry Potter and the Chamber of Secrets (2002)	876,700,000
13	Harry Potter and the Order of the Phoenix (2007)	872,646,000
14	The Lord of the Rings: The Fellowship of the Ring (2001)	871,368,364
15	Finding Nemo (2003)	864,625,978
16	Star Wars Episode III: Revenge of the Sith (2005)	850,000,000
17	Spider-Man (2002)	821,708,551
18	Independence Day (1996)	817,000,000
19	E.T. the Extra-Terrestrial (1982)	792,900,000
20	Harry Potter and the Prisoner of Azkaban (2004)	789,804,554

1. **import** openpyxl as xl

    #This imports the openpyxl module and adds an alias of xl.

2.

3. workBook = xl.load_workbook('movies.xlsx')

    #Loading the excel file

4. sheet = workBook['Sheet1']

    #Loading the specific sheet. If you do not identify the sheet, it will raise an error.

5. cell = sheet['B2']

    #Accessing a certain cell. Again it is case sensitive.

6. cell = sheet.cell(2, 2)

    #This will give you the exact same value as line 5.

7. **print**(cell.value) # Printing the value of the cell.

Program output:

```
C:\Users\...\PycharmProjects\GettingStarted\venv\Scripts\Python.exe
C:/Users/.../PycharmProjects/GettingStarted/MyFirstProgram.py
Titanic (1997)

Process finished with exit code 0
```

In the script above, we start by importing the openpyxl module and giving it an alias. This is normally done to make the code writing easier. So, instead of having to type 8 characters you will only need two. Then we continue by loading the workbook as an object in a variable, using the 'load_workbook' method with the file name of the excel sheet between double quotations. Note that the name of the file is case sensitive, so double and triple check that you have got that right, unless you are fond of errors.

Since we have the workbook loaded, we now save a specific sheet into another variable as an object – again, case sensitive. In line 5 we are calling a certain cell by placing the cell coordinates between double quotations, and yes, you guessed it, 'case sensitive'. Line 6 does exactly the same as line 5, but it uses numerical coordinates instead of the alphanumeric ones. Finally, line 7 will print out the values of a certain cell into the console.

We'll continue using the same example, but this time we'll be reading all of the contents of a certain column. We will then manipulate the values and return them in a different column, also saving it in a completely different file so that we do not make any changes to the original.

1. **import** openpyxl as xl
   #This imports the openpyxl module and adds an alias of xl.

2.

3. workBook = xl.load_workbook('movies.xlsx')
   #Loading the excel file

4. sheet = workBook['Sheet1']
   #Loading the specific sheet. If you do not identify the sheet it will raise an error.

5. cell = sheet['B2']
   #Accessing a certain cell. Again it is case sensitive.

6. cell = sheet.cell(2, 2)
   #This will give you the exact same value as line 5.

7. **print**(f'The number of rows in this sheet is, {sheet.max_row}')
Printing the number of rows in the spreadsheet.

8. **for** row **in** range(2, sheet.max_row + 1):
#Looping all of the rows in the sheet ignoring the first one.

9.   cell = sheet.cell(row, 3)
#This will save the cell information in a variable and will change with every loop.

10.   correctedGross = cell.value / 100000000

11.   **print**(f'Modifying the original value of {cell.value} to {correctedGross}') # Print the value of each cell.

12.   CorrectedGrossCell = sheet.cell(row, 4)
#The location of the new coordinates in the fourth row.

13.   CorrectedGrossCell.value = correctedGross

14.

15. workBook.save('NewMovies.xlsx')
#Saving the data in a new file.

Program output:

```
C:\Users\...\PycharmProjects\GettingStarted\venv\Scripts\Python.exe
C:/Users/.../PycharmProjects/GettingStarted/MyFirstProgram.py
The number of rows in this sheet is, 21
Modifying the original value of 1845034188 to 18.45034188
Modifying the original value of 1129219252 to 11.29219252
Modifying the original value of 1060332628 to 10.60332628
Modifying the original value of 976475550 to 9.7647555
```

```
Modifying the original value of 954782262 to 9.54782262
Modifying the original value of 924300000 to 9.243
Modifying the original value of 921600000 to 9.216
Modifying the original value of 920665658 to 9.20665658
Modifying the original value of 914700000 to 9.147
Modifying the original value of 892194397 to 8.92194397
Modifying the original value of 890065018 to 8.90065018
Modifying the original value of 876700000 to 8.767
Modifying the original value of 872646000 to 8.72646
Modifying the original value of 871368364 to 8.71368364
Modifying the original value of 864625978 to 8.64625978
Modifying the original value of 850000000 to 8.5
Modifying the original value of 821708551 to 8.21708551
Modifying the original value of 817000000 to 8.17
Modifying the original value of 792900000 to 7.929
Modifying the original value of 789804554 to 7.89804554

Process finished with exit code 0
```

In the script above, we have made a few changes to achieve our objectives. In line 10, we have calculated a modified version of the variable – note that the naming of the variables are descriptive. Then we added a print message so that we can monitor the progress on our console in line 11. Afterwards, in line 12, we created a new variable to set the new coordinates, called 'CorrectedGrossCell' - note that only the row has changed. Finally, we save the new information into the variable using the method of value (CorrectedGrossCell.value). Now that all the changes we want have been made, we terminate the program right after saving. To do that, we need to use the 'workbook.save() method while adding the name of the file between quotations along with the file extension inside of the parenthesis (example: 'workbook.save('newMovies.xlsx').

Adding Charts

To be able to add chart,s we will need to add a couple of modules from the openpyxl package. We will use the same example for this next exercise, with a few additions to it. We would like to use our newly created data to populate the values of our bar chart.

1. **import** openpyxl as xl
   #This imports the openpyxl module and adds an alias of xl.

2. **from** openpyxl.chart **import** BarChart, Reference
   #Importing the bar charts and references from the module.

3.

4. workBook = xl.load_workbook('movies.xlsx')
   #Loading the excel file

5. sheet = workBook['Sheet1']
   #Loading the specific sheet. If you do not identify the sheet it will raise an error.

6. cell = sheet['B2']
   #Accessing a certain cell. Again, it is case sensitive.

7. cell = sheet.cell(2, 2)
   #This will give you the exact same value as line 5.

8. **print**(f'the number of rows in this sheet is, {sheet.max_row}')
   #Printing the number of rows in the spreadsheet.

9. **for** row **in** range(2, sheet.max_row + 1):
   #Looping all of the rows in the sheet ignoring the first one.

```
10.   cell = sheet.cell(row, 3)
      #This will save the cell information in a variable and will
      change with every loop.

11.   correctedGross = cell.value / 100000000

12.   print(f'Modifying the original value of {cell.value} to
      {correctedGross}')  # Print the value of each cell.

13.   CorrectedGrossCell = sheet.cell(row, 4)
      #The location of the new coordinates in the fourth row.

14.   CorrectedGrossCell.value = correctedGross

15.

16. # Creating a bar chart for the modified data

17. barValues = Reference(sheet, #Referencing our data range in
    the excel sheet and saving it into a variable.

18.             min_row=2,

19.             max_row=sheet.max_row,

20.             min_col=4,

21.             max_col=4

22.             )

23. chart = BarChart()
    #Creating a bar chart instance inside of a variable.

24. chart.add_data(barValues)
    #Adding the values in the chart data.

25. sheet.add_chart(chart, 'E2')

26. print(f'Creating bar chart for {sheet.max_row -1} rows')
```

27. # Saving output to a new excel sheet

28. workBook.save('NewMovies.xlsx')

    #Saving the data in a new file.

Program output:

```
C:\Users\...\PycharmProjects\GettingStarted\venv\Scripts\Python.exe
C:/Users/.../PycharmProjects/GettingStarted/MyFirstProgram.py
The number of rows in this sheet is, 21
Modifying the original value of 1845034188 to 18.45034188
Modifying the original value of 1129219252 to 11.29219252
Modifying the original value of 1060332628 to 10.60332628
Modifying the original value of 976475550 to 9.7647555
Modifying the original value of 954782262 to 9.54782262
Modifying the original value of 924300000 to 9.243
Modifying the original value of 921600000 to 9.216
Modifying the original value of 920665658 to 9.20665658
Modifying the original value of 914700000 to 9.147
Modifying the original value of 892194397 to 8.92194397
Modifying the original value of 890065018 to 8.90065018
Modifying the original value of 876700000 to 8.767
Modifying the original value of 872646000 to 8.72646
Modifying the original value of 871368364 to 8.71368364
Modifying the original value of 864625978 to 8.64625978
Modifying the original value of 850000000 to 8.5
Modifying the original value of 821708551 to 8.21708551
Modifying the original value of 817000000 to 8.17
Modifying the original value of 792900000 to 7.929
Modifying the original value of 789804554 to 7.89804554
Creating bar chart for 20 rows

Process finished with exit code 0
```

169

The program pretty much runs the same up until line 17 where we start creating our chart. The first thing that we need to do is to reference our range of data. For that, we use the reference() function in which we can set certain parameters; the starting row as the 'min_row', the last row as max_row with a value of 'sheet.max_row' (we use this anyway since we have already calculated it), the starting column as 'min_col' and the ending column as 'max_col'.

In line 23, a bar chart instance is created using the BarChart() class and we save it in a variable. We then proceed on the next line by saving the referenced data in line 17 into the actual bar chart instance. We continue by placing the bar chart into the sheet while determining where it's top left position should be placed respectively, using the 'sheet.add()' method. The last change that we have made to this script is printing a message stating that the bar chart is being created.

Manipulating Sheets

You can create and remove sheets by using, the 'create' and 'remove' methods that come as part of the openpyxl package. In the upcoming example, we have an excel file with information about movies. Before we start creating and removing sheets, we should be able to access the sheet names. We will be using two different methods to print out our sheet names. One of them is simply adding the list information into a variable using the 'sheetnames' method in line 9. The other one is printing each sheet name individually using a loop. This is a similar method as the one used in the CSV module.

1. **import** os #This will import the os module to be able to navigate through the files of your computer.

2. **import** openpyxl as xl

    #This will import the openpyxl module to use with excel.

3.

4. thePath= os.getcwd()

    #Method of knowing what your root directory is and saving it in a variable.

5. **print**(thePath) # Printing the exact root directory

6. wb= xl.load_workbook("movies.xlsx") # loading the excel workbook.

7.

8. # Printing the worksheet names separately using a 'for loop'.

9. **print**(wb.sheetnames)

    #Printing all of your sheets in a workbook

10. **for** ws **in** wb:

11.   **print**(ws.title)

Program output:

```
C:\Users\...\PycharmProjects\GettingStarted\venv\Scripts\Python.exe
C:/Users/.../PycharmProjects/GettingStarted/MyFirstProgram.py
['Grossing', 'Adventure', 'Fantasy']
Grossing
Adventure
Fantasy

Process finished with exit code 0
```

Next, let's create a couple of sheets so that we can use them to store information in them later. We will also remove an unnecessary sheet, renaming another and saving the excel workbook in the same file.

1. **import** os
   #This will import the os module to be able to navigate through the files of your computer.

2. **import** openpyxl as xl
   #This will import the openpyxl module to use with excel.

3.

4. # Loading workbook,.

5. thePath= os.getcwd()
   #Method of knowing what your root directory is and saving it in a variable.

6. **print**(thePath) # Printing the exact root directory

7. wb= xl.load_workbook("movies.xlsx")
   #loading the excel workbook.

8.

9. # Printing worksheet names before changes.

10. sheetNames =wb.sheetnames #Using the sheetnames method.

11. **print**(f'The original sheets were: {sheetNames}')
    #Printing sheet names before changes.

12.

13. # Creating new sheets.

14. wb.create_sheet('Horror')
    #This will create the sheet after the last index.

15. wb.create_sheet(index=1,title='Comedy')
    #Create sheet with (this will show as the second sheet).

16.

17. #Removing sheets

18. wb.remove(wb['Adventure'])
    #Specifying which sheet to remove.

19.

20. # Changing worksheet name.

21. sheet2 = wb['Gross']

22. sheet2.title = 'Grossing'

23.

24. # Printing the worksheet names separately using a 'for loop'.

25. **print**(f'The updated sheets are:')

26. **for** ws **in** wb:

27.   **print**(ws.title)

28.

29. # Saving changes on the workbook

30. wb.save("movies.xlsx")
    #Saving changes to the same file. To save to a different file,
    specify a different name.

31. **print**('>>>Changes saved successfully')
    #Confirmation message for the user.

Program output:

```
C:\Users\...\PycharmProjects\GettingStarted\venv\Scripts\Python.exe
C:/Users/.../PycharmProjects/GettingStarted/MyFirstProgram.py
The original sheets were: ['Gross', 'Adventure', 'Fantasy']
The updated sheets are:
Grossing
Comedy
Fantasy
Horror
>>>Changes saved successfully

Process finished with exit code 0
```

After loading the sheet, we printed out the current sheet names in line 11. The next chunk of code in line 13 creates sheets using two different methods, either adding it at the end of the queue or specifying where to position it between the sheets. In line 17, we remove one of the sheets, 'Adventures,' by using the new statement. An old statement to remove the sheets exists. However, it will be discontinued in future versions - stick to this one. Renaming the sheets is fairly simple, as shown in lines 21 and 22. Just remember not to use any special characters that you would not be allowed to us in excel. The program then proceeds to print out the changes on the console and save the file.

Chapter 16

Using PDFs and Word Documents

These two file formats are not your traditional plain text files. They include features like formatting colors, fonts, positioning, and even the ability to turn them into an interactive form. Nevertheless, they are still binary files, and with the use of a couple of modules, we can programmatically manipulate these files.

PDF documents

In the business world, PDF documents are the standard way to portray the final output of a document. The idea is to deny readers the ability to make changes to the file, which could alter its meaning. Obviously, there are many programs that allow you to alter PDFs, and Python has a few tricks up its sleeve. We will be using a module called PyPDF2.

To install the module, click on the terminal tab found in the run tool window all the way at the bottom. We will need to type a command to download and install the module 'pip install PyPDF2'. It's a relatively small file and should take a few seconds. Once you are prompted with the success message, go back to the run tab.

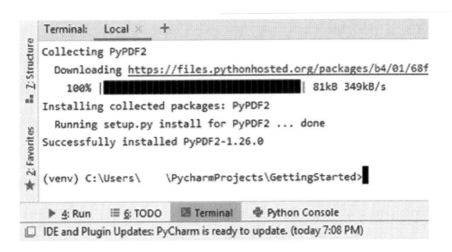

```
Terminal:   Local   ×   +

Collecting PyPDF2
    Downloading https://files.pythonhosted.org/packages/b4/01/68f
        100% |███████████████████████████████| 81kB 349kB/s
Installing collected packages: PyPDF2
    Running setup.py install for PyPDF2 ... done
Successfully installed PyPDF2-1.26.0

(venv) C:\Users\    \PycharmProjects\GettingStarted>
```

▶ 4: Run   ☰ 6: TODO   ▣ Terminal   ◈ Python Console

☐ IDE and Plugin Updates: PyCharm is ready to update. (today 7:08 PM)

One of the main issues with PDFs is that they are not easy to deal with when it comes to converting the content into text. Don't get us wrong, they are the go-to format whenever you need to print a file. However, it is not our best friend at the moment. That said, there may be cases when the module is unable to open a certain file, and unfortunately, there is not much we can do in that regard. Regardless, this particular module has been able to open all the PDFs that we have used so far, and you should not be too worried.

Extracting text from PDFs

The module that we are using does not have the ability to extract charts or images. It strictly deals with text and inserts the as a Python string.

Extracting text from a PDF is a walk in the park. We open the PDF object as we have before and then pass the text into a variable, which we can then use. Here is an example.

1. **import** PyPDF2 as pdf # Importing the PDF module.

2. pdfFile = open('Manuscript.pdf', 'rb')
    #Storing the PDF into an object in 'read binary' mode.

3. pdfReader = pdf.PdfFileReader(pdfFile)
   #This stores the total pages in a variable.

4. **print**(f'this PDF has {pdfReader.numPages} pages.')
   #Displays the number of pages within the PDF.

5.

6. pageText = pdfReader.getPage(0)
   #getting the text from the first page only.

7. **print**(pageText.extractText())
   #Printing the text to the console.

Program output:

```
C:\Users\...\PycharmProjects\GettingStarted\venv\Scripts\Python.exe
C:/Users/.../PycharmProjects/GettingStarted/MyFirstProgram.py
This PDF has 3 pages.
The Incomprehensible Script
```

Back when I was still a student at grade five one of our teachers had a discussion that marked my future. This manuscript was a beautiful piece of art with undecipherable texts that no one in the world was able to understand. It had jaw dropping drawings and tidy writing with an enchanting font. My first reaction was, this is spectacular! Then moved on to what is it about? Where our teacher said nobody knows. At this point.

```
Process finished with exit code 0
```

It is important to note that PDFs are unpredictable. In many cases, you may find line breaks and spaces in unexpected places. This can be solved programmatically, but it also may affect the text if certain breaks and spaces are intended.

Creating PDFs

Unlike other modules we have used, you only have a small set of options that you can utilize with the module. The main things that can be achieved are to copy, rotate and overlay pages, as well as encrypting and decrypting PDFs. Another limitation is that it does not allow you to edit PDFs; it only allows you to copy information and create a new file.

Copying pages

A great function that you can use Python for is combining information from PDFs into a single file. For instance, your boss asks you to combine all of the minutes of a meeting for the whole month. Doing it manually can be incredibly tedious. Luckily, we can do that with a few lines of code.

1. **import** PyPDF2 as pdf # Importing the PDF module.

2.

3. # Opening file objects

4. pdfFile1 = open('Manuscript.pdf', 'rb')
   #Opening the first pdf document.

5. pdfFile2 = open('AdamsN.pdf', 'rb')
   #Opening the first pdf document.

6.

7. # Defining reader variables.

```
8.   pdf1Reader = pdf.PdfFileReader(pdfFile1) #First PDF reader.

9.   pdf2Reader = pdf.PdfFileReader(pdfFile2)
     #Second PDF reader.

10.

11. # Setting up PDF writer.

12. pdfWriter = pdf.PdfFileWriter()

13.

14. # Creating a loop to copy all of the text from the first PDF.

15. for pageNum in range(pdf1Reader.numPages):

16.     pageText = pdf1Reader.getPage(pageNum)

17.     pdfWriter.addPage(pageText)

18.     print(f'Copying first PDF...')

19.

20. # Creating a loop to copy all of the text from the second PDF.

21. for pageNum in range(pdf2Reader.numPages):

22.     pageText = pdf2Reader.getPage(pageNum)

23.     pdfWriter.addPage(pageText)

24.     print(f'Copying Second PDF...')

25.

26. # Writing the new PDF file.

27. pdfOut = open('combine.pdf', 'wb')
     #Opening pdf file with 'write binary' access.

28. print(f'Creating combined PDFs...')
```

29. pdfWriter.write(pdfOut)

30. pdfOut.close()

31. pdfFile1.close()

32. pdfFile2.close()

Program output:

```
C:\Users\...\PycharmProjects\GettingStarted\venv\Scripts\Python.exe
C:/Users/.../PycharmProjects/GettingStarted/MyFirstProgram.py
Copying first PDF...
Copying first PDF...
Copying first PDF...
Copying Second PDF...
Copying Second PDF...
Copying Second PDF...
Creating combined PDFs...


Process finished with exit code 0
```

In the example above, we have inserted two PDFs into our program, and have included all of the objects so we are able to read the data inside of 'for loops'. We set up the PDF writer in line 12 using the pdf.PdfWriter() method. In lines 27 and 28, we open an empty PDF to save our information in. Don't worry, if you do not have an empty PDF, this module will create one for you. We end the program by closing all of the PDFs that we have opened.

Rotating pages

Another cool feature that we can use is the option to rotate PDFs by 90 degree increments using the two built-in methods. We can use the rotateClockwise() or rotateCounterClockwise() methods. This is an excellent tool when you need to rotate all of those documents the office scanner sent you in a PDF document that needs to be rotated.

1. **import** PyPDF2 as pdf # Importing the PDF module.

2.

3. # Opening file objects

4. pdfFile = open('Manuscript.pdf', 'rb')

5. pdfReader =pdf.PdfFileReader(pdfFile)

6.

7. # Inserting required page into a variable.

8. pageRotate = pdfReader.getPage(1)

9.

10. #Rotating page.

11. pageRotate.rotateClockwise(180)
    #Rotating page by 180 degrees.

12. **print**(f'Page rotated Clockwise.')

13.

14. # Writing results into a new file.

15. pdfWriter = pdf.PdfFileWriter()

16. pdfWriter.addPage((pageRotate))
    #adding the page to the new document.

17.

18. pdfOutput = open('Rotated Page.pdf', 'wb')

19. pdfWriter.write(pdfOutput)

20. **print**(f'File Saved as Rotated Page.')

21. pdfOutput.close()

22. pdfFile.close()

Program output:

```
C:\Users\...\PycharmProjects\GettingStarted\venv\Scripts\Python.exe
C:/Users/.../PycharmProjects/GettingStarted/MyFirstProgram.py
Page rotated Clockwise.
File Saved as Rotated Page.

Process finished with exit code 0
```

Overlaying pages

Overlaying pages will place them on top of one another. This is used when you need to add a logo, watermark or a header. Python has the ability to overlay pages to multiple files or certain pages on a file.

1. **import** PyPDF2 as pdf # Importing the PDF module.

2.

3. # Opening file objects

4. pdfFile = open('Manuscript.pdf', 'rb')

5. pdfReader =pdf.PdfFileReader(pdfFile)

6.

```
7.  # Inserting required page into a variable.

8.  page1 = pdfReader.getPage(1)

9.

10. pdfWateramarkReader =
    pdf.PdfFileReader(open('watermark.pdf','rb'))

11.

12. page1.mergePage(pdfWateramarkReader.getPage(0))

13.

14. # Writing results into a new file.

15. pdfWriter = pdf.PdfFileWriter()

16. pdfWriter.addPage(page1)

17.

18. for pageNum in range(1, pdfReader.numPages):

19.     pageFile = pdfReader.getPage(pageNum)

20.     pdfWriter.addPage(pageFile)

21. pdfOutput = open('brochure.pdf', 'wb')

22. pdfWriter.write(pdfOutput)

23. pdfOutput.close()

24. pdfFile.close()
```

The program starts by importing the pyPDF2 module and opening a PDF file with read binary as an argument in line 4. The program then pulls out the first page and places it into a variable. In line 10, the watermark page is opened and merged with the existing file in line 12.

Finally the watermark is written over all the desired range using a 'for loop'.

Encrypting PDFs

Encrypting a PDF does not simply mean that you will add a password to the file. The encryption process ensures to change the binary code so that it is unreadable unless the correct password is entered. There are programs that are able to crack PDFs, but they are not always successful. In this next script, you will learn how to encrypt a file.

1. **import** PyPDF2 as pdf # Importing the PDF module.

2.

3. # Opening file objects.

4. pdfFile = open('AdamsN.pdf', 'rb')

5. pdfReader = pdf.PdfFileReader(pdfFile)

6.

7. # Setting up PDF writer.

8. pdfWriter = pdf.PdfFileWriter()

9.

10. # Making a copy of the PDF.

11. **for** pageNum **in** range(pdfReader.numPages):

12.   pdfWriter.addPage(pdfReader.getPage(pageNum))

13.

14. # Encrypting the PDF file.

15. pdfWriter.encrypt('password')

16.

17. # Saving the PDF file.

18. pdfOutput = open('encryptedPDF.pdf', 'wb')

19. pdfWriter.write(pdfOutput)

20. pdfOutput.close()

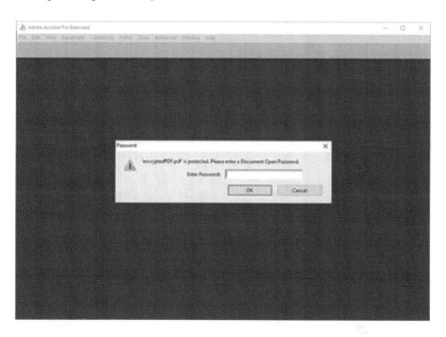

Decrypting PDFs

Some PDF files that you may work on may come encrypted. If you have the password, you can access the files normally via the module.

1. **import** PyPDF2 as pdf # Importing the PDF module.

2.

3. # Opening file objects.

4. pdfReader = pdf.PdfFileReader(open('encryptedPDF.pdf', 'rb'))

5.

6. # Verifying that the file is encrypted.

7. **print**(pdfReader.isEncrypted)

8.

9. # Decrypting the file.

10. pdfReader.decrypt('password')

11. #Reading and printing the PDF

12. pageFile = pdfReader.getPage(0)

13. **print**(pageFile.extractText())

Program output:

```
C:\Users\...\PycharmProjects\GettingStarted\venv\Scripts\Python.exe
C:/Users/.../PycharmProjects/GettingStarted/MyFirstProgram.py
True
This is the confidential document that is password protected.

Process finished with exit code 0
```

This program is set into four main stages: Opening the file, verifying that it is encrypted, decrypting the file and accessing the information inside it. If you attempt to open the file without decrypting it, Python will produce an error stating that it cannot read it. Meanwhile, if you try to decrypt a file that is not encrypted, Python will produce an error as well. This happens because the protocols of access are different, so it is important to check the status of a file before attempting to access it.

Conclusion

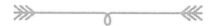

As a beginner to programming, we want to congratulate you on making it through the first steps of this wonderful journey. Now, with your feet past the threshold, we invite you to take a look at the world beyond and really let your imagination go wild. There is no limit to what you can do once you've put your mind to it.

In this book, you have been given the basics of programming using Python. You have suffered through a multitude of syntax errors, exceptions and potential system crashes. And now your eyes have been opened to the world of programming. So, where do you go from here?

The answer is simple: Go wherever the wind takes you.

At this point, you should know what it is that you want to do with your newly acquired programming skills. As the magician that you now are, you have to forge your own path and decide how to best utilize your magic. For instance, most of the Python authors' work involves using Application Program Interfaces (APIs). This means that the need to gather and process data is never-ending.

When it comes to yourself, there is nothing that can be better offered than information about what is out there for you to explore. There are many disciplines that are in need of your programming abilities. These few may help you choose which way you need to go.

187

Data scientists are in need of Python developers, as it is an extremely good tool that offers many modules to solve a lot of limitations found in other languages. However, the most important thing is how well Python developers are paid.

Machine learning is best practiced in Python, although there are other programming languages that have libraries to support it. None come close to Python, though. It is being used by corporations like Google, along with thousands of programmers around the world.

Web development using Python and Django makes it very easy to build web applications. If your passion lies there, you can do in mere minutes what it would take other developers to do in hours.

Whatever your choice, wherever the journey may take you from here, just know that you are ready to take on all the challenges you may face. We truly believe that you are armed with some of the best informational bullets we can give you, and enough tips and tricks to get you started in this world of codes. As with everything else in life, view this as an adventure, and don't be afraid to venture forth and explore new territories. There is still so much more that Python can offer, and for the programmer in you looking for more advanced techniques and tips, the world is your oyster.

So go, Young Programmer, and show the world what you can do!

Made in the USA
Middletown, DE
05 January 2021